The Art & Design Series

For beginners, students, and professionals in both fine and commercial arts, these books offer practical how-to introductions to a variety of areas in contemporary art and design.

Each illustrated volume is written by a working artist, a specialist in his or her field, and each concentrates on an individual area—from advertising layout or printmaking to interior design, painting, and cartooning, among others. Each contains information that artists will find useful in the studio, in the classroom, and in the marketplace. Among the books in the series:

Chinese Painting in Four Seasons:
A Manual of Aesthetics & Techniques
Leslie Tseng-Tseng Yu/text with Gail Schiller Tuchman

Drawing: The Creative Process
Seymour Simmons III and Marc S.A. Winer

Drawing with Pastels
Ron Lister

Graphic Illustration:
Tools & Techniques for Beginning Illustrators
Marta Thoma

Understanding Paintings:
The Elements of Composition
Frederick Malins

An Introduction to Design: Basic Ideas
and Applications for Paintings or the Printed Page
Robin Landa

Painting and Drawing: Discovering Your
Own Visual Language
Anthony Toney

A Practical Guide for Beginning Painters
Thomas Griffith

Teaching Children to Draw:
A Guide for Teachers and Parents
Marjorie Wilson and Brent Wilson

Transparent Watercolor:
Painting Methods and Materials
Inessa Derkatsch

Nature Drawing: A Tool for Learning
Clare Walker Leslie

Portrait Drawing: A Practical Guide
for Today's Artists
Lois McArdle

Robin Landa, chairperson of the art department at Elizabeth Seton College in Yonkers, New York, has received numerous awards for her excellence in drawing, painting, and teaching. She has written many articles on design, and her work has been exhibited in several major galleries in the United States.

AN INTRODUCTION TO DESIGN
basic ideas and applications for paintings or the printed page
ROBIN LANDA

A SPECTRUM BOOK

Prentice-Hall, Inc.
Englewood Cliffs, N.J. 07632

Library of Congress Cataloging in Publication Data

Landa, Robin.
  An introduction to design.

  (The Art and design series)
  "A Spectrum Book."
  Bibliography: p.
  Includes index.
  1. Design. I. Title.
NK1510.L36   1983   745.4   83-3275
ISBN 0-13-480624-7
ISBN 0-13-480616-6 (pbk.)

The Art & Design Series

© 1983 by Prentice-Hall, Inc.,
Englewood Cliffs, New Jersey 07632.

A SPECTRUM BOOK

10 9 8 7 6 5 4 3 2 1

ISBN 0-13-480624-7

ISBN 0-13-480616-6 {PBK.}

Cover design by Hal Siegel
Editorial/production supervision by Peter Jordan
Interior design and page layout by Maria Carella
Manufacturing buyers: Christine Johnston
    and Edward J. Ellis

This book is available at a special discount when ordered in
bulk quantities. Contact Prentice-Hall, Inc.,
General Publishing Division,
Special Sales, Englewood Cliffs, N.J. 07632.

Prentice-Hall International, Inc., *London*
Prentice-Hall of Australia Pty. Limited, *Sydney*
Prentice-Hall Canada Inc., *Toronto*
Prentice-Hall of India Private Limited, *New Delhi*
Prentice-Hall of Japan, Inc., *Tokyo*
Prentice-Hall of Southeast Asia Pte. Ltd., *Singapore*
Whitehall Books Limited, *Wellington, New Zealand*
Editora Prentice-Hall do Brasil Ltda., *Rio de Janeiro*

contents

preface

Although *An Introduction to Design* is written for anyone who wishes to develop an understanding of visual principles, it is most clearly intended as a text for studio art classes in two-dimensional design and color. Those of us in the art professions are fully aware that the beginning student needs a strong understanding of the fundamental design and color principles in order to pursue a career in advertising design, graphic art, illustration, or painting.

This book provides the reader with basic design and color ideas in an analytical, comprehensive form. This is not a book heavy with rhetoric or theory, but rather a clear, succinct structure with practical applications, hands-on experiences, illustrations, and critiques. In each chapter particular ideas and topics are presented that are reinforced by creative projects for the reader to execute. These projects are followed by solutions—works by professional artists relating to the topic—and a knowledge-gained section that sum-marizes the principal lesson of the project. A bridge is made between ideas and practice; empirical projects provide the reader with an irreplaceable exploration of the subject.

The book is based on a teaching philosophy that not only emphasizes creativity, but also develops intellectual skills. Design and color are presented as interdependent disciplines in which compositional ideas are stressed. The reader is made aware of the dynamic potential of design and color and the organic connections between the two subjects.

The theoretical positions that underlie the structure of this book are a result of my own work as an artist, many years of graduate study, and years of college-level teaching in design. Although the format of the book is flexible and can be adjusted to the personal needs of the individual instructor, the organization of the contents is based upon successful classroom experiences. After having completed the course upon which this book is based, students have excelled in advanced art classes and in the professional art field.

I feel this book will help people succeed in their chosen art field and those individuals in search of understanding the visual world, and will serve as a valuable classroom text to instructors.

ACKNOWLEDGMENTS

I am indebted to the many talented students from Elizabeth Seton College whose works appear in this text and whose efforts greatly added to the success of the design and color projects. Thanks also to the many artists, designers, photographers, gallery and museum officials, and organizations who so graciously contributed to this project.

Special thanks to my editor at Prentice-Hall, Mary Kennan; and the Prentice-Hall staff, especially Maria Carella, Peter Jordan, Betty Neville, and Stephanie Kiriakopoulos, with whom I worked most closely; and to Dr. Miriam Fuchs, Dr. Richard Nochimson, Dr. Walter Raubicheck, Allan Robbins, and Mary Ann Smith, who read the manuscript and offered constructive criticism.

Finally, my sincerest gratitude goes to Barbara Dodsworth, Theresa Drap, Sheila Kinnally, Julie Martinson, Renee Nyahay, Kathleen O'Connell, and Michael O'Keefe, for their invaluable assistance, advice, and encouragement.

**This book is dedicated to
my mother and father,
Betty Landa and Hyman Landa,
for their
invaluable support and love.**

one
introduction

WHAT IS DESIGN?

Design is a medium that allows us to express feelings, philosophies, and ideas and to communicate messages in a meaningful way. It is an analytical way of organizing our thoughts and translating them into a corporeal form.

Design was not born in a vacuum. It is a developed discipline that reflects the complexity and rationality of the human mind as well as our sense of ourselves in relation to the physical world. If we analyze the physical space we live in we will see the connections it has to two-dimensional design. There are verticals, horizontals, curves, diagonals, colors, textures, patterns, and shapes in the environment. These elements in the physical world have three dimensions and identities: trees, buildings, chairs, bridges, clouds. But we don't compose our two-dimensional designs through the literal identity of forms.

The formal elements in design are *line, color, shape, volume, texture, form, light,* and *shadow*. Formally, trees and their branches are verticals with diagonal extensions in relation to the horizontal lines of the earth. It is through a formal rather than a literal language that we compose. We look for formal relationships among elements, the way a vertical relates to a curve or the way a red relates to a green. For example, a painter might see a bunch of apples as a series of overlapping curves. A typographer might see a series of words as different black and white shapes. This is a formal approach to seeing, an analytical approach. It is this way of seeing elements and interactions that we, as designers, must attempt to control and analyze.

Very often design is perceptually derived, taken from images seen in the real world. But design can also be conceptual, stemming from inventions of the mind. It can be abstract, using formal elements that do not directly relate to identifiable objects, or it can be representational, describing or depicting images from the real world.

The purpose of design is to stimulate our perceptions. Mediums that incorporate design, such as painting, drawing, printmaking, and photography, serve no purpose other than to activate our minds, senses, and spirits. Advertising art, although it utilizes the same design principles, has a singular purpose: to sell ideas, products, or services.

Design is a fascinating medium that can be studied and mastered.

THE MATERIALS

The basic materials for an exploration of two-dimensional design are simple. In the preliminary stages of any design we do what are called *thumbnail sketches*. These are small, rough, quick design ideas. Any sketch pad, tracing pad, or visualizer pad is fine. Some designers prefer working out ideas on tracing paper or visualizer paper because it allows them to quickly trace parts of a design. Thin and thick black felt-tipped markers are wonderful for working out design ideas on a small scale. Drawing pencils may be used; they range in lead hardness from 9H (lightest value) to 6B (darkest value), which is the softest.

Finished designs will be executed in any of the following materials:

PAINT
• Tempera
• Casein
• Acrylic paint in the following colors: red, yellow, blue, green, black, and white

(Note that oil paints take too long to dry for the purposes of these exercises and watercolors are too transparent.)

COLOR PAPERS & ILLUSTRATION BOARDS
• 1 Color-Aid pack of assorted precolored papers
• Illustration boards: hot press (smooth) in white and gray

TOOLS
• 1 small pointed sabeline brush

• 1 flat ¼-inch bristle brush
• 1 flat ¾-inch bristle brush
• Disposable palette
• Matte medium for acrylics or casein paint
• Rubber cement
• Rubber cement pickup
• Scissors, x-acto knife, or single-edged razor blades
• Steel ruler
• Compass
• Black drafting or charting tape, ¼-inch wide and/or ½-inch wide
• Triangle (optional)
• T-square (optional)
• Typeface catalog (optional)

THE SYSTEM & THE PROCESS

The aim of this text is to reveal to the reader/student the organic nature of two-dimensional design. Design is a rational system of composing parts into a coherent whole. Therefore, composition is the key element in design, and composition will be stressed in every chapter of the text. The chapters are organized thematically, and we are expected to bring the knowledge gained in each chapter to each successive chapter. The concepts and projects in later chapters depend upon those in the early chapters.

Each chapter contains projects: design experiments. There is no substitute for empirical knowledge. Execution of the projects and an analysis of the experience will provide an invaluable understanding of design fundamentals.

In order to successfully execute the projects the reader should consider the following working process:

1. Understand the project. Redefine the exercise in your own words. Do not lose sight of the aim of the project. It is very easy to create a beautiful solution that does not answer the problem.
2. Do many thumbnail sketches. (See Fig-

1-1 Thumbnail sketches
Mary Ann Smith, designer, New York
These are thumbnail sketches for
Project 8-4, *The Common Object.*
Thumbnail sketches are small,
quick designs done to work out ideas.

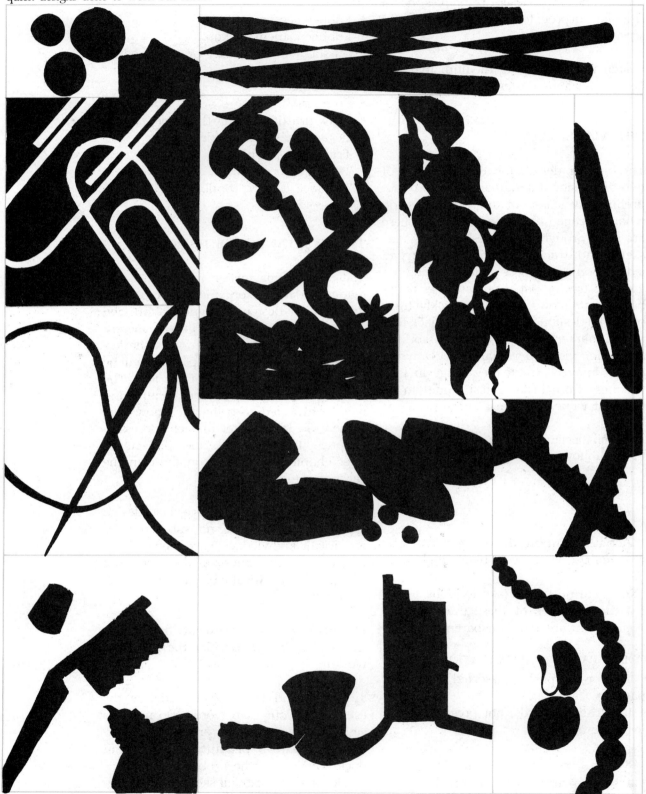

ure 1.1.) Do not lock yourself into one answer too quickly. If you cannot work out your ideas on a small scale beforehand then work them out on a larger scale, but be open to any changes or new ideas that might occur.

3. Ask yourself the following questions: Have I analyzed my solutions? Am I on target? Is my solution a cliché? Have I pushed the solution as far as I can?

4. The last step is to take your idea and execute it neatly and professionally. Sloppiness and haste detract from good ideas.

**two
color**

how can we define it? how can we begin to gain control over it?

Color is at once the most mysterious, complex, and yet deeply communicative of all subjects. Its illusive nature must be studied and defined, and even then it can be controlled only by a practiced and educated eye. Of course, some people have a marvelous intuitive sense of color, but the educated eye understands and is able to see through color's many facades and weights. By combining the study of color with design we realize the interdependence of color with form, volume, and placement.

There have been many scientific studies of color, and a knowledge of them is useful to our understanding of color phenomena. But most of what we need to know about color will come from practical experimentation. This empirically derived knowledge will enable us to develop methods of using and seeing color that may easily be broadened to more and more complex levels.

We can discuss, study, measure, and identify color more specifically if we divide the concept of color into three different qualities: *hue, value,* and *chroma.* Separating these qualities allows us to learn about them individually and to gain a working control over them. Controlling these aspects of color is essential to a knowledge of design, painting, and advertising art.

We will try to build a vocabulary of visual experience so that our sense of color can grow as our responses to perception, intuition, and active seeing grow. We will also try not to be stifled by locking ourselves into only one scientific theory or a particular level of taste.

Hue: Hue is the specific name of a color: blue or red, green or orange. The word *hue* means the name of the color. A color may have a simple name, such as green, red, or blue, or a compound name, such as blue-green.

8

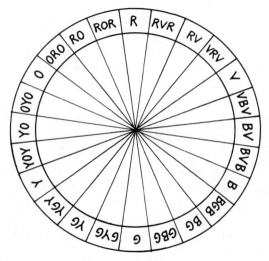

2-1 *The Geometric Color Wheel*
The geometric color wheel is a
circular band of hues from
which we can derive many color
theories and harmonies. The painter's
primary colors—red, yellow, and blue—
traditionally stem from this wheel.
We can also locate the secondary
colors—orange, green, and violet.
Between the primary colors and
secondary colors are the compound
colors. Between the compound colors
and either the primaries or secondaries
are the complex compound colors.

Value: Value refers to the relative lightness
or darkness of a hue. We can have a light
red or a dark red, a light blue-violet or a
dark blue-violet. Some hues are inherently
lighter in their pure state than others. For
example, yellow right out of the tube is
close in value to white, whereas blue right
out of the tube is closer to black.

Chroma: Chroma refers to the relative
intensity of a hue, whether it is bright or
dull, weak or strong. Hues differ by nature
in their chromatic intensities. Orange is
inherently much brighter than blue. It is
important to note that all colors do not
have the same value at their highest point
of intensity. For example, the brightest
yellow is much lighter in value than the
brightest blue.

This system of nomenclature enables us to
refer specifically to colors and communicate more clearly. Names such as *brown,
fuchsia,* or *powder blue* are fashion terms
and are too ambiguous to help us conduct
a thorough investigation of color.

THE PAINTER'S PRIMARY COLORS

When Sir Isaac Newton passed white light
through a prism, the light was transformed into the colors of the spectrum. He
then took the colors that appeared and
formed them into a continuous band of
color which we call the *geometric color
wheel.*

The painter's primary colors, red, yellow,
and blue, traditionally stem from the
geometric color wheel. They correspond in
pigment to cadmium red, cadmium yellow, and ultramarine blue. These hues are
essentially pure. They contain no other
hues. For example, a pure red would not
appear to contain blue or yellow. A pure
yellow would not appear greenish or
reddish.

SYSTEMS FOR MEASURING & IDENTIFYING HUE, VALUE, & CHROMA

Hues can be arranged along the circumfer-
ence of a sphere, or on a flat geometric
wheel. The geometric color wheel was
popular in the nineteenth century and
remains so today because it affords a clear
system of ordering hues and finding many
possible color harmonies.

Red, Yellow, Blue: Primary colors that
cannot be mixed from any other color in
pigment.

Orange, Green, Violet: Secondary colors
that are each a mixture of two of the
primaries.

*Red-Violet, Blue-Violet, Orange-Red, Yel-
low-Orange, Yellow-Green, Blue-Green:*
Compound hues that are each a mixture
between primaries and secondaries.

*Red-Violet-Red, Blue-Violet-Blue, Violet-
Red-Violet, Violet-Blue-Violet, Orange-Red-
Orange, Yellow-Orange-Yellow, Red-*

9

Orange-Red, Orange-Yellow-Orange, Yellow-Green-Yellow, Blue-Green-Blue, Green-Yellow-Green, Green-Blue-Green: Complex compounds that are mixtures of compounds with either primaries or secondaries. There can be as many complex compounds between hues as the subtlety of pigment will allow.

We can refer to these hues by the first letters of their names: Red = R, red-orange = RO, and orange-red-orange = ORO.

Red and Green, Blue and Orange, Yellow and Violet: examples of colors that are opposite each other on the geometric color wheel. They are *complements.* When they are mixed together in pigment, they produce a gray hue. This neutralization of hue occurs when equal amounts are added together. The complements must be adjusted to equal values before they can completely nullify each other. Complements can have different types of relationships depending upon placement, size, scale, type of pigment, or paper. We will explore these relationships at a later point.

All colors are affected by their surroundings. In fact, the color that our eye perceives is completely dependent upon all surrounding conditions, including the type of light and other colors. We cannot be sure that all normal healthy eyes read a color exactly the same. We have little biological control over our perception, but as trained colorists we can make adjustments based on known facts about the relative nature of color.

Josef Albers, a noted teacher and color theoretician, emphasizes the idea that color is the most relative medium in art. The hue of a color can be changed by altering its surroundings. For example, if we place a small square of violet, which we will call the *key*, in the middle of a larger blue square, which we will call the *ground*, it will appear to be a red-violet. This occurs, as repeated experimentation will show, as a result of subtraction. Any ground subtracts its own hue from hues placed on it and therefore influences the appearance of the key hue. Violet is a mixture of blue and red; therefore, the blue subtracts itself from the violet and leaves the red to visually dominate the mixture.[1] Primary hues cannot be changed in this way because they are not mixtures of any other pigments. Only hues that are mixtures or compounds can be altered in hue by their surroundings. The appearance of primary hues, however, can be changed in terms of value and chroma. Any ground subtracts its own value or chroma from the key color placed upon it and therefore influences it. For example, a middle-value red can be made to appear lighter by placing it on a dark ground and vice versa.

[1]This information is based on the teachings of Josef Albers, the author of *The Interaction of Color*. (New Haven: Yale University Press, 1963).

hue differences

MATERIALS
- Color-Aid pack
- 9-inch-square illustration board
- Cutting tool
- Rubber cement
- H pencil

1. Rule the 9-inch square into nine equal sections.
2. Select eight different hues that all have red in them and arrange them on the grid.
3. Place a true or pure red in the center of the grid as a control hue.
4. Color-Aid, paint, or magazine clippings can be used.
5. Compare all chosen hues to the pure red to see if they are truly hue mixtures and not value variations of the pure hue. Can you identify the differences?
6. Do the same for blue, green, and violet.

Knowledge Gained
We all have differing notions of color names. If someone asked a group of people to think of the color blue each person would probably think of a different blue. Some would think of a blue with green in it; some would think of a blue with red in it; some would think of "navy" blue, others cobalt, others ultramarine, and others thalo blue. Which person would be correct?

It really is not a matter of being correct or incorrect, but of being able to see the subtle differences among all the variations. The more distinctions we are able to make, the more possibilities we have at our fingertips.

Just as there is a color wheel to determine hue, there is a vertical scale to determine relative gradations of value from white to black. Newspapers, magazines, film, video, and television are black and white mediums that have trained our eyes to see a limited number of contrasting grays because of the inherent limits of the printing process. There are innumerable grays in nature and the artist's palette is more suited to capturing these grays than even the most expensive printing process. Inevitably, works by painters that use a subtle palette of grays mixed from colors (not black and white) reproduce in much higher contrast as a result of the limits of the printing process. Take an expensive full-color-process reproduction of a Corot to the museum and hold it up to the original. You will be amazed at the level of heightened contrast in the print.

We must train ourselves to see beyond the limitations of the mediums that have trained our vision from early childhood. Our aim in the investigation of value is to train our eyes to comprehend very subtle and minute shifts in light and dark. Value is perhaps the hardest quality of color to read because it is obscured by hue and chromatic intensity. Bright hues jar our retinas, making it difficult to judge accurately a color's true value. Determining value is something that has to be practiced. We can do this by comparing the value of bright hues to those values that are easier to read, such as values mixed from black and white. If we create a scale of grays that range from near white to near black we will begin to learn how to measure value gradations.

11

gray scale

MATERIALS
- Black and white tempera paint
- Blank index cards
- Brush

1. Spread 25 index cards on a flat surface.
2. Begin mixing by adding a small amount of black paint on your palette to a larger amount of white paint.
3. Cover one end of a card with this original mixture.
4. Continue mixing small amounts of black into the white, and after every addition cover a side of an index card.
5. Work quickly and try to move toward a near black range at the end.
6. Notice that there may be a deficiency in a certain value range. If this observation is made early the needed area can be filled in. Note that many areas will appear to look the same even though more black was added to the mixture. This is because at a certain point the amount added to the mixture must increase in order to effect a visual change.
7. Choose a 10-step scale out of the 50 painted swatches.
8. *Choosing the 10 steps*
    a. First choose a near white and a near black step. Place them at opposite ends in a vertical line.
    b. Then choose a middle-value gray, which is step 5.
    c. Then choose value steps 2, 3, 4, 6, 7,

8, and 9 by comparing them with the first three choices. Overlapping the values will allow you to make a better decision.
d. Make sure that they move in equal steps, as though they were steps on a staircase. No one step should be steeper than another.
e. Cut the final selections into 1-inch squares, neatly mounting them on a 10-by-1-inch vertical strip of illustration board. You can then use this as a kind of ruler of value.

Knowledge Gained
Although this may seem to be a tedious task, the experience is invaluable. Learning to discern small changes in value is something that takes work and time. Note that it is easier to read the value of a gray mixed from black and white because there is a lack of intensity. It is much more difficult to read the value of a pure red because it is by nature an intense color. If you have trouble determining the value of an intense color, it might be beneficial to compare it to your gray scale. It also might be helpful to attempt mixing value scales in different hues: a scale of light red to dark red or light yellow to dark yellow. This type of palette experience trains us to read value; and reading value is the key to good color judgments.

2-2 Student Work, *Gray Scale*
The gray scale should move in even steps from a near white step to a near black step. The ability to read values accurately is crucial to the use of color.

hue scales

MATERIALS

- Magazines
- Illustration board
- Cutting tool
- Rubber cement

1. Find reds, yellows, and blues from magazines and other precolored papers that match your gray scale in a 10-inch step range.

2. What does a dark yellow look like? Dark yellow, dark orange, and dark red are generally called brown. But there are many different browns that derive from various high-intensity hues such as orange, red, yellow, yellow-orange, red-orange, red-violet, and other combinations.

Knowledge Gained

Comparing high-intensity hues against the gray scale will train our eyes to make sound value judgments. If there is difficulty in reading the particular value of a high-intensity hue, begin by slightly overlapping the bright hue on the first step of the gray scale. Then slowly slide the bright hue down the scale until you find the value that seems closest to it. Squinting our eyes helps us to read value.

It is necessary to isolate the three qualities of color in order to learn how to read them accurately. If we were to paint from life, we would have to make color decisions based on these investigations. It is much more difficult to make good decisions when confronted with a varied arrangement of colors. Therefore, the more we are able to discern the different qualities of color the less confusing it will be when we are confronted by complex situations.

All hues have a range of chromatic intensity. They can be manipulated to appear duller or brighter. This change can occur in visual perception by virtue of placement and surroundings. A hue's chromatic intensity can be shifted by physically mixing the pigment with specific hues. Remember that colors differ by nature in their chromatic strength, some being much more powerful than others. As we have said, orange is much brighter than blue in their pure states or right out of the tube.

There are various methods of changing the chroma of a hue. Some colors, such as red and yellow, are *opaque;* they come out of the tube at their highest intensity. Some colors, such as ultramarine blue or alizarin crimson, are *transparent* and need a small amount of white added to them to reach their highest intensity. Lowering the chroma of a hue is more complicated. In a later chapter we will explore two possible ways through color mixture. We can affect the chroma of a color, just as we can visually alter the appearance of a hue or a value, by surrounding the chroma with another hue or placing it next to another hue. We can make use of complements to create a chromatic optical mixture. Complementary colors are opposites on the color wheel and they carry with them certain inalienable properties. They have the ability to enhance one another or nullify one another by creating a visual gray.

The discovery of *optical mixture,* or the mixing of a color in our visual perception, led to the painting techniques of the Impressionists and Post-Impressionists, particularly of the Pointillists. They were prompted by the writings of color theoreticians and artists such as Charles Henry and Eugène Delacroix, who felt that colors would retain their purity if they mixed

13

visually rather than physically. When pigment is added to pigment the mixture becomes progressively more inert.

Our eyes behave in ways that we cannot fully control no matter how educated our vision becomes. We experience phenomena such as after-image and optical mixture.

AFTER-IMAGE

Scientists believe that the human eye has color receptors that are sensitive to the primary colors red, yellow, and blue, which constitute all colors. If we stare at blue we will exhaust the blue receptor and be left with red and yellow, which produce orange. Orange is the after-image of blue.

The same is true for the other two receptors. Red produces a green (blue + yellow) after-image; yellow leaves a violet (red + blue) after-image; and blue produces an orange (red + yellow) after-image.

OPTICAL MIXTURE

At a certain distance, small strokes of colors will visually merge and produce the sensation of a single new color. For example, if we place small dots of yellow and blue next to one another, from a certain distance the two colors will appear to be green. If we place small dots of red and green, which are complements, next to one another, they will visually merge at a distance and appear gray. In this case the red and green annul one another and form a third color, gray.

chromatic recession & advancement: a warp

MATERIALS
- Color-Aid pack
- Illustration board
- Cutting tool
- Rubber cement

1. Select a pair of complements.
2. Find all the light values, middle values, and dark values of the pair of chosen complements in the pack.
3. Alternate the complements, to achieve a warp. The pairing of the complements in different values and intensities will make the surface of the board appear to swell and recede. (See Project 4-4.) Relative distances from the surface can be achieved by manipulating values and chromas.

Make sure that the strips of paper are thin enough at some points to allow for optical mixtures to take place and wide enough at other points for the complements to enhance one another.

Knowledge Gained

We have pushed and pulled hues into different appearances through the complementary relationship. We have allowed our perception to work for us through optical mixture. We have also created space by allowing intense hues to come forward and duller hues to recede. Remember that the duller hues should be a result of optical mixture rather than of using low-intensity papers.

15

three
the container

what are our limits?

As designers we must first understand our limits. The limits in design are what define it as a medium: line, shape, texture, tone, color, space, and so on. The simple limits in two-dimensional design are the borders of the page, which we will call the *container*.

Most often the container is a rectangle made up of two horizontals and two verticals. Artists have used rectangular containers since the Renaissance and, of course, the page in advertising is a rectangle as well. The rectangle carries with it certain relational properties; if we understand these relationships we can easily translate similar principles that apply to differently shaped containers.

All elements within the container interact with its particular overall shape. As soon as we make a single mark on the page, that mark reacts to the container's borders and creates the internal space. If we think of the rectangle as two vertical lines and two horizontal lines that are joined at right angles, then the first mark or line that we draw is actually the fifth line. The line or mark we have made either reinforces the container or contrasts with it.

• Any mark or line we set down on a page is basically either a repeat of the container's borders or a counterpoint to it.
• Any mark or line begins to define the internal space and the quality of that space. For example, the space may be deep space or frontal space.
• Any mark or line is either static or dynamic in relation to the container and in relation to other marks or lines.

Static and dynamic elements are relative to the original container shape.(See Figure 3-2 on p. 22.)

RECTANGULAR CONTAINERS: SQUARES & REGULAR RECTANGLES
• Verticals and horizontals are static within a rectangle.
• Diagonals and curves are dynamic within a rectangle.

18

3-1a Nicolas Poussin, *The Feeding of the Child Jupiter*, oil on canvas
Courtesy of the National Gallery of Art, Washington, D.C. (Samuel H. Kress Collection)
A *regular rectangle* is not extremely prolonged in any direction. This regular rectangle is held horizontally to accommodate the narrative and multiple figures.

3-1b American Broadcasting Companies, Inc. 1979 annual report
Aubrey Balkind, art director,
Philip Gips, Diana Graham, designers,
Gips & Balkind & Associates, Inc., New York
Corporate literature is usually in the form of a *regular rectangle* held vertically. Depending upon the composition of the design, the container can be thought of as a vertical extension. This design uses the container as a *regular rectangle*. We are made to feel that the container is actually larger than it is because the letters *abc* are at an angle and are curvilinear. The angle and contrasts in the photograph give the container power.

3-1c Raphael, *The Alba Madonna*, paint on canvas
Courtesy of the National Gallery of Art, Washington, D.C. (Andrew W. Mellon Collection)
A *tondo* is a circular container. The tondo is particularly appropriate to the theme of the Madonna and Child because it completely embraces the imagery. A tondo is an all-embracing perfect unit.

3-1d Franz Kline, *Horizontal Rust*, 1960, oil on canvas
Courtesy of the Sidney Janis Gallery, New York

This container is called a *vertical extension*. It is extremely prolonged in a vertical direction. Vertical extensions can give a sense of divisions, such as heaven, earth, and hell or sky, land, and water. The vertical extension can be used to communicate an extended field of vision. It can symbolically express a move from bottom to top or top to bottom, as well as expressing a sense of continuity of extended space. The brushstrokes in *Horizontal Rust* boldly move our eyes up the extended vertical field.

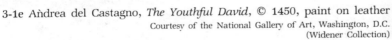

3-1e Aǹdrea del Castagno, *The Youthful David*, © 1450, paint on leather
Courtesy of the National Gallery of Art, Washington, D.C.
(Widener Collection)

Artists have used many different shapes and surfaces as containers since the beginning of art. This image of David with the head of Goliath is painted on a leather shield which was probably carried in processions in the fifteenth century. Aǹdrea del Castagno makes full use of the diagonal sides of this shaped container by countering them with a strong internal diagonal: the arm of David. David's legs are also at opposing angles to the sides of the container.

3-1f Edgar Degas, *Before the Ballet*, oil on canvas
Courtesy of the National Gallery of Art, Washington, D.C.
(Widener Collection)

Degas chose a *horizontal extension* as the container for *Before the Ballet* to communicate movement in time. We follow the gestures of the dancers across the extended field and relate the movement to the idea that dance is unfolded in time. It is as if time unfolded in a horizontal direction.

3-1g Jack Reilly, *Rhythm in Flux*, 1981,
acrylic on canvas
Courtesy of the Aaron Berman Gallery, New York
Many contemporary artists feel that the arena of painting can be greatly extended through the use of shaped canvases. Movement is established in the container itself as well as in the internal space of the container.

3-1h Piet Mondrian, *Diagonal Composition*, 1921,
oil on canvas
Courtesy of the Sidney Janis Gallery, New York
Mondrian, in his mature works, did not use diagonals within his compositions. But he did use diagonally held containers, which gave a different set of properties to his internal verticals and horizontals.

3-1i Tom Wesselmann, *Smoker #27*, 1980,
oil on canvas
Courtesy of the Sidney Janis Gallery, New York
Shaped canvases can have geometric edges or flowing curved edges. Wesselmann uses the shape of the container to express the organic quality of the smoke.

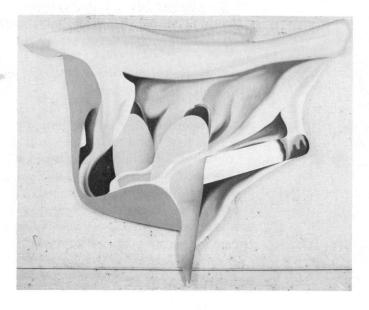

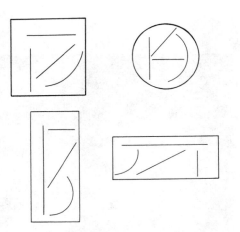

3-2 Diagram of static and dynamic elements in different containers.

TONDO

- Curves are static within tondos.
- Verticals and horizontals are dynamic within tondos.
- Diagonals are dynamic within tondos.

VERTICAL EXTENSIONS: PROLONGED VERTICAL RECTANGLES

- Horizontals are static within a vertical extension.
- Diagonals and curves are dynamic within a vertical extension.
- Verticals are dynamic within a vertical extension due to the fact that they are repeating an exaggerated edge.

HORIZONTAL EXTENSIONS: PROLONGED HORIZONTAL RECTANGLES

- Verticals are static within a horizontal extension.
- Diagonals and curves are dynamic within a horizontal extension.
- Horizontals are dynamic within a horizontal extension due to the fact that they are repeating an exaggerated edge.

All elements are responsive to the original shape of the container.

The statement that certain lines are static and others dynamic in relation to the container is of course conditional We are able to create tensions within a regular rectangle through the use of verticals and horizontals. But we must vary the distances between the lines and/or the thickness of the lines in order to make verticals and horizontals dynamic within a regular rectangle. It is up to us to constantly be aware of how elements react to one another and to the container. This analytical process allows us to investigate the character of the container.

We understand design elements by virtue of relationships and differences. For example, Nicolas Poussin, a seventeenth-century painter, set up a series of diagonal counterpoints in the painting *The Rape of the Sabine Women*. Literally, rape is about struggle; formally, within the design medium, the struggle or violence is expressed as one diagonal counterpointing another. Our visual entry into the painting occurs diagonally across the ground plane from the left corner under the figure of Romulus on the platform to the extreme right background. If we stand to the left of the painting the space opens up on either side of the diagonal entry. The architecture in the background is based on ancient architecture and sets up static verticals and horizontals against which we feel the power of the diagonals. The violence is felt by virtue of its design; the facial expressions and body gestures are the human elements hung over the design skeleton.

The container is the container of meaning. The design elements take on particular levels of feeling and cause responses when they are considered in relation to the container. Advertisements, book jackets, or packages that set their imagery or headlines at a diagonal in relation to a rectangular container are gaining a powerful impact on the viewer because of the relationship of diagonals enclosed by verticals and horizontals. It is a quick and powerful statement. The direction of the lines within the container affects the viewer. A designer's choice of container is significant in relation to the particular message that designer has in mind. If we become aware of design as a thinking process and a process of decision making, we can allow these principles to become a part of an acquired vocabulary. Just as in the use of language, certain structures become second nature to us.

3-3 Nicolas Poussin,
The Rape of the Sabine Women,
oil on canvas
Courtesy of The Metropolitan Museum of
Art, New York
(Harris Brisbane Dick Fund)
A rape is literally about struggle.
The rape is expressed formally
within the design medium as
counterpointing diagonals within a
regular rectangle. Counterpointing
diagonals are extremely powerful
and express violence against the
original horizontals and verticals
that comprise the container's
edges.

3-4 *Aero-Flow Dynamics*
Eugene Grossman, art director,
Don Bartels, designer,
Anspack Grossman Portugal, Inc., New York
The title of this corporate literature is set as a diagonal within
a rectangular container. It is read quickly and is dynamic
because of its placement.

3-5 Champion International Corporation, *Champions of the Future*
appointment calendar cover, 1981
Bruce Blackburn, design director, Danne & Blackburn, Inc., New York
Depth is created through the use of a title set at an extreme
diagonal to the container. The gradual shift in value from dark to
light in the type, as well as the gradual reduction in the size
of the letters, increases the illusion of depth. The dynamic
move into space is appropriate to the idea of the future.

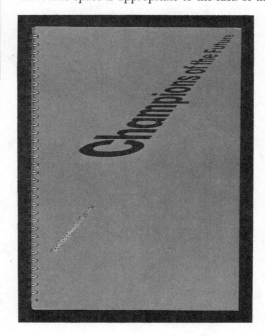

defining the container

MATERIALS
- Ruler
- Pencil or marker
- Drawing pad

1. Rule a series of four rectangles, each 4 inches by 5 inches, on a drawing pad.
2. Within the first rectangular container draw a shape that will activate the surface.
3. On the next two rectangular containers draw shapes that will activate the entire surface.
4. On the fourth rectangular container draw all three shapes, so that the entire container is utilized. You may trace them in actual size or reduce and arrange them.
5. Make sure that both the internal space and the edges are activated.
6. Rule four vertical extensions, each 6 inches by 3 inches, and proceed in the same way.
7. Rule four horizontal extensions, each 3 inches by 6 inches, and do the same thing.
8. Draw four tondos, each 5 inches in diameter, and repeat the process.

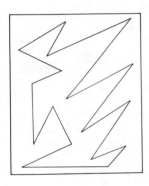
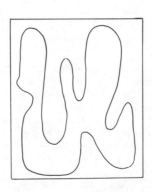

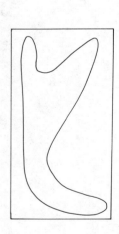
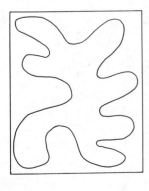

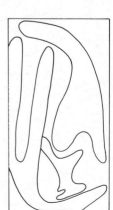

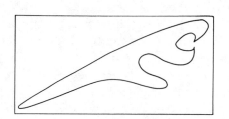

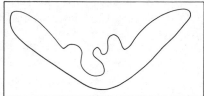

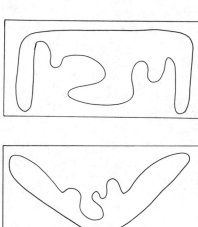

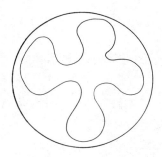

Student Work, *Defining the Container*

3-6a (opposite page, far left)
In order to activate the container, the entire space and the shape of the container must be considered. Notice that, in most cases, the edges of the drawn shape form shapes with the edges of the containers. Composing the three shapes in the different types of containers must be a thoughtful process. We must ask ourselves whether we are thinking of the entire space at all times. All shapes within the container affect all the other shapes as well as the internal space.

3-6b (opposite page, near left)
The shapes in these vertical extensions tend to be vertically elongated to activate the entire space. In composing the three shapes together, the artist has one curved shape react to another curved shape to form a kind of implied oval.

3-6c (this page, top)
The composition of the shapes in the horizontal extension seem to overlap one another, creating interesting shapes between the shapes.

3-6d (left)
The overlapping of the shapes in the tondo tends to give the container internal volume.

25

Knowledge Gained

We tend to forget that the container is a full participant in the overall graphic message. The imagery is not the only element to be considered. The container is not a mere frame but an important design element. The act of engaging the container should be a major part of the design process. It is easy for us to engage the container's energies when that is the sole aim and we are drawing only one shape. The purpose of combining all three shapes is to introduce complexity in the form of multiple elements and to force compositional thinking. Composition is a process that goes on in drawing, painting, layout, and pure design and also includes related arts such as writing, music, sculpture, and architecture. Composition may be defined as the general structural arrangement of a work. It corresponds to the definition of the container because it is ultimately the process in which we make use of the container. Whether we create deep space or stay on the surface, use color or black and white, we must try to be responsible to the particular container. Be aware of the properties and the potential of the container, and *think compositionally!*

3-7 Judith Stockman and Associates, stationery
Bill Bonnel, art director & designer,
Bonnell & Crosby, Inc., New York
The three simple geometric shapes positioned on the stationery, envelope, and business card all activate their respective containers. It is not necessary to draw all over a page in order to activate the space. The spacing between the three shapes by Bill Bonnell is tense because of the position of the shapes and the way they seem to communicate with one another.

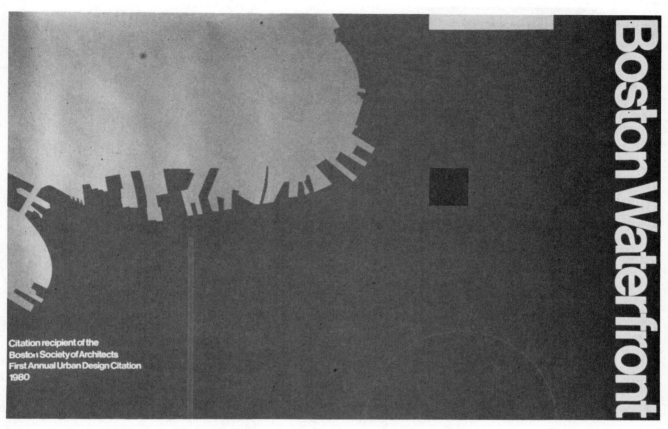

3-8 Boston Society of Architects, Boston Waterfront poster
John Massey, art director & designer, Container Corporation of America, Chicago
The empty space seems to have great energy due to the composition of
the very different shapes. All edges of the container are considered and activated.

3-9 Advanced Micro Devices, Annual Report, 1980
Lawrence Bender, art director
Linda Brandon & Lawrence Bender, designers,
Lawrence Bender & Associates,
Palo Alto, California
Four different hues, one on each edge, define
the borders of the container. Three thoughtfully
positioned lines activate the entire space.
The page is so acutely sensitive that simple
lines immediately engage the space and
create interesting tensions. Incidentally,
the four hues are red, orange, green, and
violet and the major space is gray. The bright
hues vibrate against the gray center and
once again call attention to the defined borders.

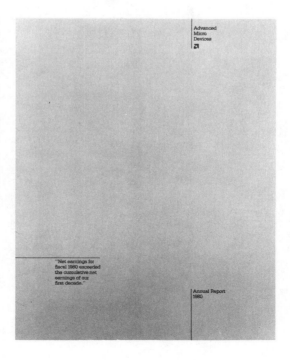

27

clarinet

cello

sarah the doll lady

charlie

oh
she's one of the
you know all my dolls *are favorites*
but people haven't got the money
some of them pay it out in *two*
three payments
i let them
they get the doll when they have it paid out
and i'm here *seven days a week*
and if i *don't* have a bench
i have a *chair* with me
what can i do
i try so hard
i'm doing this for so many years
eh

you couldn't ask for anything less than what you ask for

do you have relatives out here?
i'm the *oldest* in my family
they're all dying before me

yeah

the *times* began it
and they *all followed*
they *all* came around
and they *buy* dolls from me too
i made a *man doll*
a french doll
witha *sequin hat*
and *everybody* wants one
but i haven't been able
i was so mixed up with the funeral
and my husband
i *can't tell you* how i suffered
so what could i do?
i *suffered* while he was *alive*

expressively
mf

i'm tellin' you
i'm very nice to people
people *appreciate me*
the *newspapers* write *beautiful* stories about me

oh yeah   local papers and the

3-10 (facing page) *Versations*, book
Warren Lehrer, author, art director, designer,
& typographer, Jan Baker & Wentao Cheng,
Letterers, Stamford, Connecticut,
Lehrer/Baker, Publisher
This container is a horizontal extension.
Mr. Lehrer designs the type and shapes
to activate the entire span of the prolonged
rectangle. Our eyes are directed by an
intriguing and unpredictable layout.

3-11 Champion International Corporation,
Champions of the Future
appointment calendar, 1981
Bruce Blackburn, design director, Danne &
Blackburn, Inc., New York
The thoughtful placement of four rectangular
photos at the left side of the page engages the
entire container. The horizontal lines of
type on the left-hand page relates the composition
to the lay-out of the right-hand page.

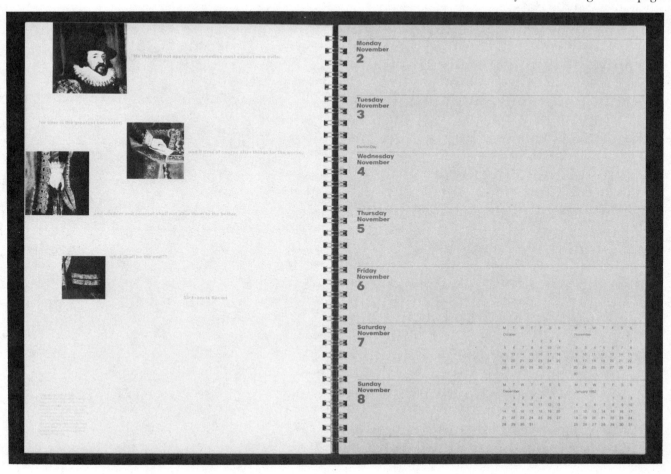

**four
an investigation
of the surface
through line**

how can we affect the surface?

We know intellectually and physically that the surface exists; we can feel it and see it. It is a two-dimensional surface that is affected by changing attitudes. You may deal with the same two-dimensional surface in different ways. If you write on a page, it's flat; if you draw on it, it's dimensional.

There is a surface, but it is shifted by illusions. Illusions can be set up with the simple element of *line*. Line, one of the designer's most fundamental elements, has many characteristics. It can be edge or it can just be movement. It can tie up the surface and make us feel its inherent flatness or it can create the illusion of space or a surface shift.

When we draw lines we don't draw what we see perceptually; we are expressing our sense of touch. There is a fundamental human need to leave one's mark. Children often trace their hands for precisely this reason. It proves their existence to them. The outline is proof of their physicality.

The use of line or outline in Renaissance painting expresses tactility and acts to connect and suspend forms in time. This linear element in painting is highly artificial; lines do not exist in nature as carriers of form, yet we readily accept and respond to their use in painting and drawing. We do not see outlines around people or forms in real life, yet we have come to understand lines as important compositional and volumetric tools.

Lines have reactive energies. They react within the given element of the container. Lines can be dynamic in relationship to one another. Their dynamics are based on

- Their relative thickness
- Their relative distance from one another
- Their placement in the container
- Whether they are broken or continuous
- Whether they are central or touching the edges of the container

Dynamics are primarily set up through differences.

4-1 Bridget Riley, *Ochre, Cerise & Turquoise Twisted Curve, Blue Dominant*, 1976
gouache on paper
Courtesy of the Sidney Janis Gallery, New York
Bridget Riley's work is considered to be an integral part of the Op Art Movement. Op Art is short for *optical art*, art that is involved with perceptual games and illusion. The curving lines Riley paints on the flat surface certainly convince the viewer that the surface has shifts and is not flat. The variation in the thickness and color of the lines adds to the swells that appear to exist. The variation in the line also lends to the appearance of continual movement.

4.2 Sandro Botticelli,
The Birth of Venus, oil on canvas
Courtesy of the Uffizi Gallery, Florence, Italy
Botticelli uses line as the carrier of the forms in this painting. The line holds and suspends all the forms close to the surface. Although there is some sense of depth, the use of a horizontal line as the horizon and the use of line to describe the forms continually make us aware of the forward space. The line sets up organic connections in terms of the composition and we feel internal rhythms as our path of vision follows the line. The line also appeals to our sense of touch by reinforcing edges and connections between forms.

4-3 Sandro Botticelli, *Primavera*,
panel painting
Courtesy of the Uffizi Gallery, Florence, Italy
We do not see lines around forms. We see by virtue of light and shadow, but we accept the use of line in art as a valid method of depicting reality. Its use in the Renaissance is probably far removed from its use today, but we should realize that line is a powerful compositional tool no matter what its symbolic meaning is. Botticelli's linear movement is harmonious and lyrical, creating connections among forms, repeats, and rhythms.

4-4 Arshile Gorky, *Organization,* © 1932,
oil on canvas
Courtesy of the Sidney Janis Gallery, New York
The line in this painting organizes and
connects all the forms and shapes. The
line also becomes edges for different shapes and
forms. The line is the compositional organizer.

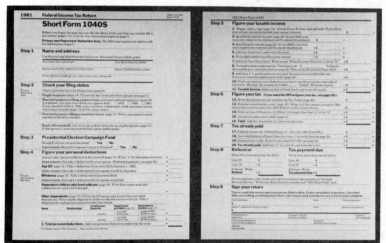

4-5 *Proposed IRS Income Tax Form*
Ann Breaznell, art director & designer
Siegel & Gale, New York
Lines that do not extend across the entire
surface of the page and that are varied in value
appear to have different positions in space.
The dark lines and large, dark type appear to
be in front of the lighter lines and smaller,
lighter type in space. This variation in
light and dark, as well as the variation in type
scale, creates space. The space created is
shallow because the lines, although not fully
extended across the page, do act to tie up
the surface.

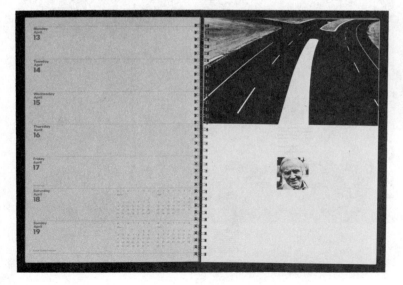

4-6 Champion International Corporation,
Champions of the Future, appointment calendar,
1981
Bruce Blackburn, design director, Danne &
Blackburn, Inc., New York
The slightly curving white lines seem to bend
the surface of the page. The central wide
white line brings our eye movement both up and
back down to the central focus of the photo.

surface space

MATERIALS
- Drawing pencils
- Ruler
- Eraser
- 2 white 10-inch-square illustration boards

1. By drawing lines of the same thickness completely across the page, varying only the distances between the lines, try to create a feeling of swelling or warping of the surface. Affect the surface in such a way that it appears to have a tangible presence.

2. By varying the thicknesses of lines, set up rhythms and vary the speed of eye movement across the page. Lines must be drawn completely across the page.

Knowledge Gained

The first exercise defines the surface: you have physically changed the look of the surface by virtue of horizontals. The second exercise introduces dynamics by degree of variation: dark lines vs. light lines, "fast" areas vs. "slow" areas. We have now seen that space can exist very close to the surface of the page. We have made the page swell and recede by virtue of very few elements: horizontal lines of the same weight and horizontal lines of varying thicknesses. These effects are optical illusions; obviously the page has not physically changed. When we stand at the foot of a skyscraper and look up to the top, the building seems to lean forward as if it were warped. This, too, is an optical illusion. The ancient Greeks tilted their buildings inward to avoid this illusion. Illusion does not occur only at the surface, but at all levels of space.

Let us now return to the fact that the page is inherently flat. We can appreciate the

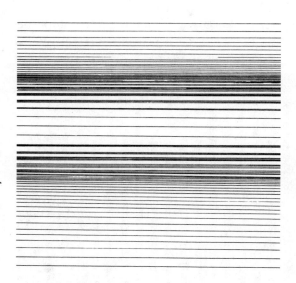

4-7 Student Work, *Surface Space*
The areas where the lines are closer together seem to recede, and the areas that are more open seem to bulge forward. It is the variation in the distance between the lines that sets up the appearance of a warp on the surface. We no longer feel that the surface is one continuous flat plane.

4-8 Student Work, *Surface Space*
We have now added another element: thickness. The dynamics have increased because we can vary the thicknesses of the lines as well as the distance between them. We can create a more dramatic shift because of the ability to set up extreme contrasts with this added element.

35

flatness now in contrast to the illusion just created. Verticals and horizontals repeat the given edges of the rectangular container. You have empirically felt the potential of horizontals, but what happens when verticals are included to stop the horizontal forces? Tensions are felt when every line established or drawn is met and stopped by an opposing line. Using the Dutch painter Mondrian as a prototype, we will show how the surface of the page may be tied up to realize its inherent flatness. We will not literally tie up the surface with string, but the vertical and horizontal lines will act like string in the way in which they will bring our eye to the surface and give the surface force and energy.

4-9 Bridget Riley, *Cartoon for Untitled Painting*, 1975, gouache on paper
Courtesy of the Sidney Janis Gallery, New York
The center of this work seems to expand and contract because of the variation in value. The thicknesses of the lines seem to change, but it is actually an optical illusion. It is the value that changes from the center to the edges.

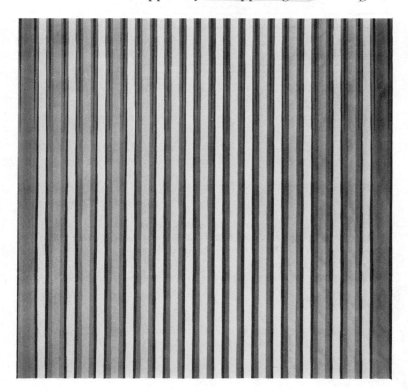

4-10 Piet Mondrian, *Composition in Red, Yellow, and Blue*, 1939–42, oil on canvas
Courtesy of the Sidney Janis Gallery, New York
Verticals and horizontals are static within regular rectangular containers, but they can be activated and energized depending upon their relationships to one another and to the container. Mondrian sets up verticals that meet and interrupt horizontals. They actively divide the surface and tie up the picture plane. It is as if string were actually wrapped around the canvas.
Although there is open white space, we do not read the space too far away from the surface. We read the white space on the same flat plane as the hues and black lines.

4-11 Édouard Manet, *Gare Saint-Lazare*, oil on canvas
Courtesy of the National Gallery of Art, Washington, D.C.
(gift of Horace Havemeyer)
The vertical poles in this painting act as a back
wall that pushes the figures forward in space.
The verticals tie up the surface, and create a
rhythmical pulse across which our eyes travel, and
the vertical emphasis tends to flatten the space.

37

opposing energies

MATERIALS
- ¼-inch black drafting tape
- Cutting tool
- 10-inch-square white illustration board

1. Using the ¼-inch black tape, set down verticals that are confronted by horizontals, displaying varying force and energy based on the distribution of lines.

2. Every line must be stopped by another line. There are to be no corners or unstopped lines.

3. The width of the tape may be varied.

Knowledge Gained

The space we have established is "up front" space. There can be an intense variation in surface energy, depending upon relative thickness of the lines, the spacing, and the rhythms that have been set up.

Everything around us has underlying structure. Do we experience an archway differently from a regular doorway? Does a domed ceiling feel different from a flat ceiling? Do we ever think of ourselves as verticals in relation to the horizontal lines of the earth? Feelings about lines come from our bodies and environments.

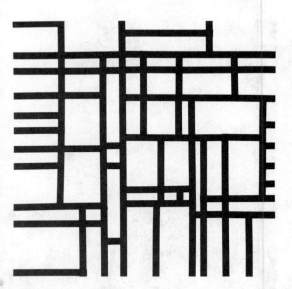

4-12 Student Work, *Opposing Energies*
When the verticals and horizontals are different in length, the rhythms are less predictable and take a longer time to read because we do not know what type of relationship our eyes will encounter as they move across the surface. Some areas seem to be slower because of their openness and others faster because they are more closely tied.

underlying structure

MATERIALS

• Charcoal sticks
• Eraser
• Rectangular paper

1. Choose a room in your home or school and on a sheet of paper record all the verticals and horizontals you see. Do not close up any forms. Merely allow them to exist as abstract forces of line.

2. After setting up the verticals and horizontals, look for diagonals and curves, constantly seeing and measuring one element against another.

3. Draw a large oval close to the edges of your structural design so that all the lines you set down originally in relation to the rectangle are now responding to the oval.

4. Rethink the design in relation to the oval.

Knowledge Gained

You have looked at real solid objects in a real environment and have extracted lines that correspond to the things seen. This ability to extract basic elements out of a real environment and transfer them to an artificial medium leads to an understanding of line as the carrier of meaning and form. By imposing an oval on your previously rectangular composition you have seen different types of lines shift from static to dynamic and vice versa.

4-14 Piet Mondrian, *Composition in Oval*, 1915, oil
Courtesy of the Sidney Janis Gallery, New York
The verticals and horizontals are architectural in spirit. Each line seems to hinge on the next as we move vertically through the space. The dark horizontals react very dynamically in relation to the oval container. Note that Mondrian sets up two vertical columns that are divided by the dark horizontals. The two vertical columns are positioned to incorporate the entire oval container.

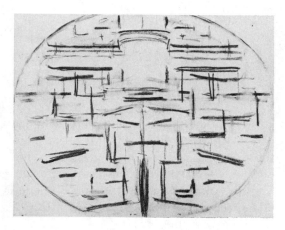

4-13 Piet *Mondrian, Pier and Ocean*, 1914, charcoal and india ink on paper
Courtesy of the Sidney Janis Gallery, New York
Mondrian establishes a vertical axis in the center of the oval container out of which he counters horizontals. The drawing is almost symmetrical and yet we feel great variation on the surface. Some horizontal lines as well as the vertical axis at the bottom of the oval are darkened to act as accents. The accented lines hold the lighter lines in place.

39

surface warp

MATERIALS
- ¼-inch and ½-inch black tape
- Pencil
- Cutting tool
- 10-inch-square white illustration board

1. Using the black tape, begin at the edge of the square with horizontal lines. Bend those lines into curves or angles of varying degrees to warp the surface of the page. The line must return to the opposite edge of the page as a horizontal. The width of the tape may be varied.

2. We may choose not to bend the line at all but to create a warp by virtue of overlapping horizontals.

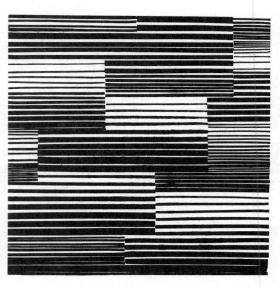

4-16 Student Work, *Surface Warp*
The sets of horizontals create slight shifts in the surface space. The space appears to be slightly layered, with one set of horizontals overlapping another.

Knowledge Gained

This project directly corresponds to Project 4-1, but goes farther in terms of the introduction of angles and curves. These angles and curves are felt intensely because they are seen in relation to their horizontal beginnings on the page.

Shallow space has great graphic impact. It immediately engages our attention and never lets the attention wane. Lines on the surface can express our sense of tactility and can also affect the surface so that it seems too far away to touch. Understanding and internalizing the basic premise that the surface is flat is vital to the creation of space. Any line drawn on a sheet of paper raises questions about its surface and potential space.

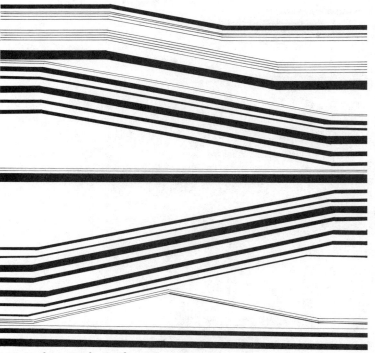

4-15 Student Work, *Surface Warp*
The use of angles to create a warp bends the appearance of the surface.

4-17 The Alden Company, *Stationary*
Robert Cipriani, art director & designer,
Michael Orzech, artist,
Gunn Association, Boston, Mass.
The concept of creating a warp in the surface
by the use of line is appropriate to the
function of the company, which produces quality
raised printing. The change in the thickness
of the line in the "raised" portion
increases the warp effect.

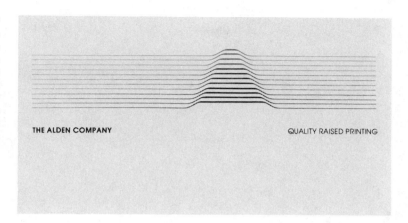

4-18 *Bloomingdale's Norma Kamali's
Super Stripes*
Palma Kolansky, photographer,
Darrell Beasley, art director
As we experienced in Project 4.4, dynamics are
set up through differences. The action in
this photograph is set up through the
juxtaposition of horizontal lines against
diagonal counterpoints. The horizontal lines
behind the figure push it forward so that
we encounter the form with immediate impact.

41

five
the creation
of volumetric
space

5-1 Master of the Barbarini Panels,
Presentation of the Virgin, oil on panel
Courtesy of the Museum of Fine Arts, Boston
(Charles Potter Kling Fund)
The use of perspective in the Renaissance
expressed the notion of control and order. The
angle moving toward the vanishing point
created depth and denied the flat surface of
the canvas.

what happens when an angle encounters a plane?

We can appreciate the inherent flatness of the page; it is a surface. It is called the *picture plane.* If we create tensions on the page that tie up the surface plane, we reiterate its natural state or concreteness. As soon as we hint at the existence of a three-dimensional space by creating a warp or drawing geometric planes on the page, we are dealing with illusion. Illusion can be created in a variety of ways: angles, warps, atmosphere, perspective, and color.

At different points in the history of art the idea of volumetric space on a flat surface has held very different meanings. The Renaissance viewed it as a reflection of the true physical nature of the world. This use of volumetric space was ordered, based on a rational system called *perspective:*

The belief that one could represent a man in a real setting and calculate his position and arrange figures in a demonstrably harmonious order, expressed symbolically a new idea about man's place in the scheme of things and man's control over his own destiny.[1]

The early twentieth century held a much dimmer view of volumetric space, thinking it was false and deceptive. The integrity of the picture plane came to be valued, and artists felt that it should not be broken. The surface was flat and should be respected as such.

It is not important for us, at this point, to make qualitative judgments about recessional space. It is, however, important to understand that the illusion or volumetric space has in the past reflected philosophies and has had different associations. At this point in art we are free to deny or create space. Contemporary artists have all avenues of artistic philosophy open to them.

The use of the diagonal on the page

[1]Kenneth Clark, *Civilisation* (New York: Harper & Row, Pub. 1969), p. 99.

44

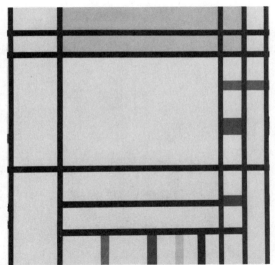

5-2 Piet Mondrian, *Place de la Concorde*, 1938–43, oil on canvas
Courtesy of the Sidney Janis Gallery, New York
Mondrian's opposing energies tie up the surface of the picture plane and reiterate the flat reality of the two-dimensional surface.

immediately raises the question of space that exists behind the surface, or perhaps in front of the surface. The angle penetrates the picture plane and brings our eye and mind to another dimension. When diagonals are linked with verticals and horizontals they form shapes which can become planes or surfaces. Planes that move diagonally create volumetric space. These planes can move in back of or in front of the picture plane. This volume has varying effects according to how the space organizes itself:

• The space can be shallow or deep.
• The planes can link up or float without touching the container or one another.
• The space can be read as pure movement, with no subject matter.
• Planes can read rationally, imitating the true physical world.
• Planes can move in relation to one another and only be understood amid themselves within their own spatial system.

Al Held, an American contemporary painter, sets up ambiguous spatial systems of geometric planes. The forms he creates can only be understood within their own relational universe. They do not directly imitate the viewer's space. Movement can evolve from the depth that these recessional planes create or the composition can remain firmly fixed in space. Raphael, an Italian Renaissance painter, sets up a completely logical and comprehensible world of depth through the use of diagonals and planes in his perspective system. His art is representational. The illusions he creates are based on things plainly visible in the true physical world.

As designers of space we must constantly be aware of the position of the picture plane, the surface of the page. In early Renaissance painting, all space and movement occurred from the picture plane back, as though the viewer were looking through a window. Various artists in the Baroque era challenged the picture plane by moving forms both in front of and in back of the picture plane, creating a heightened dramatic spatial move. Movement in front of the picture plane engages the viewer's space. The picture plane can also act as the back wall, as opposed to the idea that it is the forward window; all forms may seem to move forward from it, creating a remarkable illusion.

5-3 Al Held, B/W V, 1967–68, Acrylic on canvas,
Al Held, Courtesy of the André Emmerich Gallery, New York
Al Held's volumetric forms are described by line. The volumes support one another and are understood in relation to one another. We have no sense of where the forms are located in space other than by virtue of their relationships to one another.

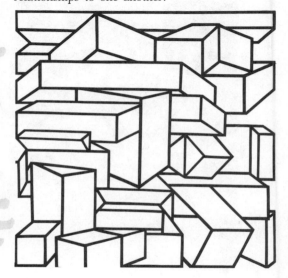

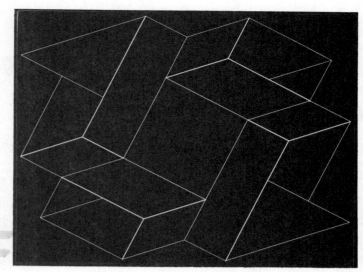

5-4 Josef Albers, *Structural Constellation*
Courtesy of the Sidney Janis Gallery, New York
The slight variation in the weight of the white lines sets up dynamics and increases the illusion of three-dimensionality.

5-5 Pieter Paul Rubens, *Prometheus Bound*, oil on canvas
Courtesy of the Philadelphia Museum of Art,
Philadelphia (W.P. Wilstach Collection)
Prometheus is set at an angle to the picture plane and our eye moves dynamically into the space. Not only are the diagonals of the figure and the bird dynamic in relation to the rectangular container, but they also create a concave space above themselves and behind the picture plane.

5-6 William Harnett, *My Gems*, oil on wood
Courtesy of the National Gallery of Art, Washington, D.C.
(Gift of the Avalon Foundation)
The front surface of the table is the established picture plane so that the sheet music moves in front of the picture plane into the viewer's space. This type of illusion is called *trompe l'oeil*, from the French for "fool-the-eye." This illusion tricks the viewer into believing that the sheet music extends in front of the picture plane. The back wall is not clearly defined. We move back into space beginning with the front plane of the table in the position of the picture plane.

the picture plane

MATERIALS
- Black and gray paper
- 2 white 10-by-12-inch illustration boards
- Cutting tool
- Rubber cement

PART I

1. Set up a still life on a table in front of a wall.

2. Using cut paper shapes and the white of the board compose and design the space and shapes you see in the still life.

3. Begin with the back wall as your first shape, using the gray paper.

4. The back wall is now in the position of the picture plane. All objects will be in front of the back wall and in front of the picture plane.

5. You might reserve large areas of black for those things closest to you in space.

PART II

1. Using cut paper shapes and the white of the second board compose and design the space and shapes you see in the still life.

2. Begin with the front plane of the table as your first shape.

3. The front plane of the table is now in the position of the picture plane. All objects will be behind the front plane or picture plane.

Do the two images differ?

Knowledge Gained

Should we be conscious of the position of the picture plane? How does the particular position of the picture plane affect the outcome of the design?

The position of the picture plane determines the type of space in the design. Space behind the picture plane affects the viewer differently from space in front of it.

One is not better than the other, but each has different effects and meanings. The position of the picture plane also tells the viewer something about the position of the artist.

This concept is an extremely abstract one; an understanding of the position of the picture plane comes through studying and analyzing great paintings and designs, as well as through empirical experience at manipulating the picture plane. Comprehending the notion of depth allows the designer the freedom to move about in more than a two-dimensional direction and to evoke different notions of reality and space. Space permits a variety of different messages to be communicated.

5-7 Levolor Lorentzen, *Levolor*,
Lyndhurst, New Jersey
The Levolor blind is the established picture plane and the figure and furniture move forward toward the viewer. The Levolor blind becomes the point of focus because of its position in space. Incidentally, this advertisement is also well designed in terms of color. The chair, the man's tie, and the word *Levolor* are all in orange-red, which moves the viewer's eye around the entire space.

5-8 Édouard Manet, *The Plum*, 1877,
oil on Canvas,

Courtesy of the National Gallery of Art, Washington, D.C.
(Collection of Mr. & Mrs. Paul Mellon)

The edge of the marble table is parallel with
the picture plane. Our eyes are directed
across the table surface, which is at an angle
to the picture plane and which creates
recessional space. Although we are given a back
wall, our entry into the space begins with
the front plane of the table and moves quickly
across the angled surface of the table.

5-9 Jean Metzinger, *Cubist Landscape*,
1911, oil on canvas

Courtesy of the Sidney Janis Gallery, New York

The entire landscape is thought of as volumes
in motion. This is not a rational perspectival
space; it is deliberately disjointed to
demonstrate the idea of constant motion and
shifting space that we encounter
perceptually in nature.

5-10 Paul Cézanne, *Houses in Provence*,
oil on canvas

Courtesy of the National Gallery of Art, Washington, D.C.
(Collection of Mr. & Mrs. Paul Mellon)

Our eyes move across the sloping plane until
we encounter the volumetric houses. The
definite geometry of the houses increases
their volume.

volumetric space

MATERIALS
- 10-inch-square illustration board
- Ruler
- H pencil
- Cutting tool
- ¼-inch black drafting tape

1. On a 10-inch-square illustration board rule a 1-inch-square grid with an H pencil.
2. Using black tape create geometric volumes and planes to affect the space.
3. You may move vertically and horizontally along the ruled lines. Diagonals may only be drawn from corner to corner of the ruled grid so that a rational perspective is maintained.
4. The use of the entire container increases the amount of believability and volume.
5. Avoid creating flat shapes and completely linear elements. Although planes are made up of linear elements—that is, lines as opposed to planes of value—they do create a believable volumetric space.
6. Be conscious of the scale of the shapes.

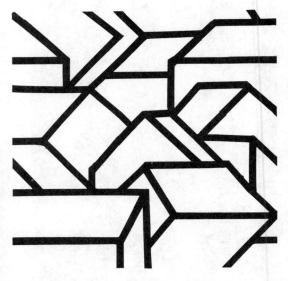

5-12 Student Work, *Volumetric Space*
This project has excellent scale. The size of the volumes in relation to one another and in relation to the size of the container makes us feel that the container is huge. The forms are bold and large. It is quite difficult to make small containers seem large.

Will you use large forms against smaller forms or keep them consistent in size? Scale may be defined as the size of forms in relation to one another as well as in relation to the size of the container. Scale is an important factor in the creation of space.
7. As you establish forms, recognize where they are in relation to the next form you set down. Have the second or third forms shifted the position of the first? of the picture plane?

Note: You may preplan your design on sketch paper or do the design directly on the board. The use of the tape allows you to easily remove and change your steps.

Knowledge Gained
The creation of volumetric space raises several important issues:

5-11 Student Work, *Volumetric Space*
This artist overlaps volumes to progressively move our eyes back into space.

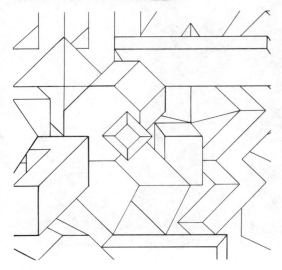

- The existence of the picture plane
- The position of the picture plane
- The creation of space behind the surface by means of diagonals
- The definition of space itself
- Scale

All forms are soon seen to be highly dependent upon one another for their position in space. The illusion created by linear volumes is very powerful and convincing, but its effectiveness does depend upon a successful use of placement and the container. The forms inside the container must react to its scale and shape. They must, most importantly, react to each other as though depending upon one another for existence.

You are working within a small container. The size of the forms within will determine scale and may imply a scale larger than the real dimensions of the container.

5-13 Juan Van Der Hamen y Léon, *Still Life*, 1627
Courtesy of the National Gallery of Art, Washington, D.C. (Samuel H. Kress Collection)
This artist clearly establishes the picture plane as the first parallel surface that we encounter. The objects placed on this shelf create a *trompe l'oeil* effect. The objects are small in scale in relation to the volumetric shelves and to the container. The light and shadow create a dramatic mood and the cast shadows push the first volumetric shelf forward. The cast shadows also encourage the illusion of three-dimensional objects on a two-dimensional surface.

5-14 Giovanni Battista Rosso, *Dead Christ with Angels*, oil on panel
Courtesy of the Museum of Fine Arts, Boston (Charles P. Kling Fund)
The size of the body of Christ in relation to the container
increases the drama of the subject. Christ's body is
compressed and takes up the entire space of the container.
His scale is large in relation to the size of the
container and makes us feel that the canvas is much larger than
it actually is. Notice that the figure's knees seem to move
forward of the picture plane.

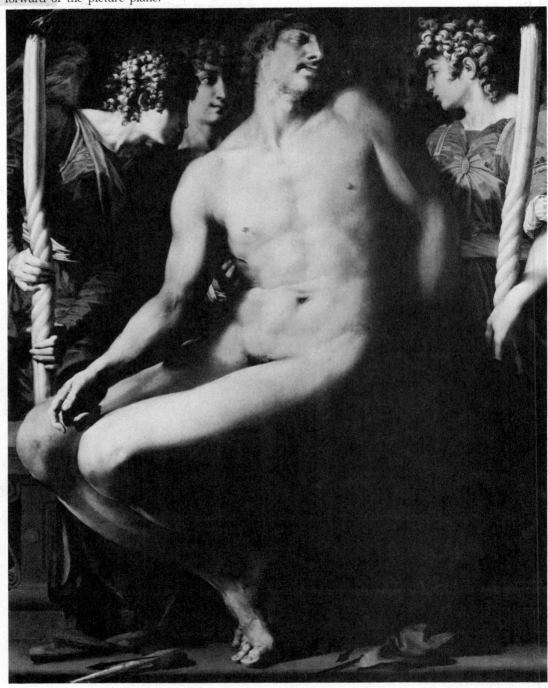

52

5-15 Christian Dior, *Teint Dior*
Christian Dior Perfumes, Inc.
The figure is spatially understood in relation to
the diagonal volume and to the edges of the container.

Christian Dior
MAQUILLAGE

TEINT DIOR Moisturizing Makeup
New interpretations of skin tones in 8 colour-perfected
shades are formulated in a moisturizing makeup,
effortlessly light and natural looking under any light,
day or night. Teint Dior is tested under medical
supervision for optimum performance.

**six
balance &
symmetry**

can we achieve balance without symmetry?

There is a built-in multiformity in balance. Balance calls forth factors such as visual weight, symmetry, gravity, placement, and direction: right and left, top and bottom. The composition of weights, meaning forms, shapes, and colors within the container, yields either balance or imbalance. The original container becomes the holder of all elements. It is the unit that either maintains its original balance or loses it because of internal forces we have created within it.

Although we have an intuitive sense of balance because it is an extension of our physical selves, we must investigate its translation into the design medium of two dimensions. We understand a great deal about balance from our physical environments and from our own psyches. We strive for balance in many aspects of our lives: in our meals, mental states, education, finances, and decors. When we arrange furniture and fixtures within a room we make decisions about visual weight and placement. At times we are so sensitive to placement that we change the position of a couch or vase for hours until it is "right." It is difficult to escape the hypnotic effect of balance in our lives.

Our innate sense of balance functions on the page in the form of symmetrical design. We seem to want to create a force and then counteract it with an equal and opposite force.

Symmetry: identical mirror images or elements arranged on either side of an imaginary vertical axis.

Essentially, the page is composed of the same and equal parts on both sides. Can we achieve pictorial balance without symmetry? Yes, asymmetrical balance can be achieved through thoughtful composition. Different elements can be placed on either side of an imaginary vertical axis to create balance. As an expression of order and harmony, balance is used deliberately to convey a message about ourselves and our philosophies. Many Renaissance artists

This painting is not symmetrical, but it is balanced. The Madonna is a vertical axis and the rounded arch over her head forms an embracing curve and a balancing force. The weight of the child's body on our right is balanced by the volume of the Madonna's arm. Her arms enfold the child in an implied oval which reinforces the embracing action of the arch above her.

This High Renaissance painting is balanced but not symmetrical. The three figures surrounding the Christ child form an inwardly curving niche. All the figures are at angles to the picture plane. The only element parallel to the picture plane is the front plane of the table, which is the established picture plane.

used balance, either symmetrical or asymmetrical, as an extension of their beliefs about people and their universe. During the Italian Renaissance there was a general belief in harmony, order, perfection, and rationality. Balance represented a stable state and harmonious proportion.

How can we achieve balance without the use of symmetry? It might be easy to balance two different pictorial elements against each other. But what happens when we introduce multiplicity through figures, objects, architecture, or simple abstract forms? Placement is the answer. We must be aware of the particular position forms occupy relative to other forms and to the container.

In visual perception different areas of the container appear to carry more or less visual weight. For instance, the center of the container is extremely powerful, but the top edge, generally, must carry less weight than the bottom to result in balance. If we were to reverse a painting that is balanced and asymmetrical, we might find that it does not maintain its balance when we exchange the elements on the left and right.

The visual weight of forms is important in achieving balance. Visual weight is understood by comparative looking. Ask yourself, does one form appear to visually weigh more than another? It might appear heavier because of its value, chroma, size, or shape. For example, two people might weigh exactly the same but appear to look quite different. Of course, two-dimensional pictorial elements are almost without physical weight; the decision-making process is based on a studied analysis of appearance.

6-3 *Versations*, book
Warren Lehrer, author, art director, designer, & typographer, Jan Baker and Wentao Cheng, letterers, Stamford, Connecticut, Lehrer/Baker, publisher
The flush-right side of the type in the center of the page is an axis for the counterpointing curves established by the positioning of the type on the opposite sides of the page. It is this underlying structure that composes the page.

6-4 Édouard Manet, *Bar at the Folies-Bergère*, oil on canvas

The barmaid is the vertical axis in this balanced composition. Manet sets up visual ambiguity in the mirror behind the barmaid. The barmaid's reflection and the reflection of a customer are seen on the viewer's right side of the painting. Which forms on the viewer's left counterbalance the two reflected images on the right? Notice that the two white circular light reflections are not evenly positioned. The white circular light on the viewer's left helps maintain the balance along with the reflection of the chandelier and other small light and dark contrasts. The predominant use of verticals and horizontals stabilizes the composition.

6-5 The Pottery Barn, *The Christmas Barn*, promotional literature
Marjorie Katz, art director, Marjorie Katz & Carol Zimmerman, designers, Marjorie Katz Design, Inc., New York
The major diagonal impulse created by the striped stocking and picked up in the form of the duck is counterpointed and balanced by the diagonally positioned word *Christmas*. The three horizontals stabilize the page and the candy cane in the upper right corner reinforces the vertical boundary; in the opposite corner, candles reinforce the vertical boundary of the container.

6-6 The Pottery Barn, *The Pottery Barn Salutes the New Classics*, magazine advertisement
Marjorie Katz, art director & designer Marjorie Katz Design, Inc., New York
In most cases, advertising designers must arrange many different elements and make the advertisement clear and cohesive. Since the copy refers to "The Classics," the use of a vertical and horizontal arrangement is appropriate. Classical design does not usually challenge the picture plane and incorporates many static elements as balancing and harmonizing elements.

6-7 Margaret Beaudette, New York, *Oval Forms*, 1980, watercolor on paper Our initiative sense of balance usually requires that the larger and broader forms be at the bottom of the page. This might be due to our natural sense of gravity. Even in this image, where we get a floating sensation, the larger forms are set at the bottom.

6-8 Barbara Dodsworth, calligrapher, New York Letterers, typographers, and calligraphers must understand balance. If imbalance is used in a design, it should be purposeful and appropriate. We tend to expect letter forms to be balanced.

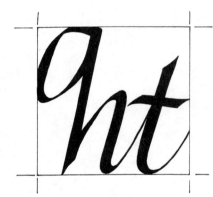

6-9 Chanel Inc., *Chanel*, 1978, magazine advertisement as seen in *Vogue*, March 1978, pp. 34-35. The letter forms in the word "Chanel" and the black product packages form a stable base for the tilted and leaning objects. Because a stable horizontal and vertical base is established, the elements that are diagonal and curved are very dynamic within the container.

retain balance &
destroy symmetry

MATERIALS

* Black and white tempera paint
* 3 10-inch-square illustration boards
* ½-inch bristle brush
* Pointed brush
* Rubber cement
* Ruler
* H pencil
* Cutting tool

1. Design the same symmetrical image on two of the three square boards, utilizing two or three simple flat geometric shapes. Fill in shapes with black paint and make corrections with the white paint.

2. Then cut one of the boards into 1-inch strips and in half down the center, yielding 20 pieces that are 1 inch by 5 inches.

3. On the third board, repaste the pieces with rubber cement, breaking the symmetry of the original image but retaining the balance.

4. The pieces must be placed back into their original slots, but their position in the slot may be shifted or reversed or cropped or eliminated. In other words, a piece from the lower right must stay in the lower right slot. It may not be placed anywhere else.

Note: Your first impulse may be to create another symmetrical image. Let your intuitive sense of balance rule you but check your decisions. Look at the asymmetrical image from a distance. Sometimes one piece in a corner will hold up a falling section. If you change one part you cause a redistribution of energies. The container and its internal elements are highly sensitive to placement; readjusting one part may lead to a readjustment of every other part.

Knowledge Gained

We understand the difference between balance and imbalance, symmetry and asymmetry. The lack of balance within a composition or design should be purposeful and deliberate. Imbalance, like balance, suggests a message or philosophy. The achievement of balance rests on the interdependence of internal elements and the container; the composition is more powerful than its separate parts. The black shapes can be arranged to activate the white space of the container. Designing this composition so that it activates space allows us to use our intuitive sense of balance as well as to train ourselves to read the weight of pictorial elements and assess the inherent properties or forces of the page. Balance can be achieved through the distribution of shapes, values, and forms within a container. Color can create balance as well. Every quality of color plays a role in the creation of balance and, of course, the result is linked directly to placement, amount, and form. There are general ideas that we must keep in mind when orchestrating color into balanced compositions:

* As with black and white, we must be able to read the weight of a color.
* A color's qualities, its hue, value, and chroma, will determine its weight.
* The relationship between the designed shape and form of a color, including its size, scale, placement, and relationship to all other colors in the composition, will determine its role in achieving balance.

For example, we may have composed a balanced design in black and white that we would like to transfer into color. We first use low chroma and different-valued hues. We then decide to introduce a bright medium-value red. The placement of that red within the composition may or may not retain the balance. The red's difference from the other hues and chromas might cause an imbalance. Placing the bright red in the center, which is a powerful position within the field, might retain the balance. If we place it in an off-center position we might have to counteract it by lowering the chroma and value of other hues at different points in the design. It is difficult if not impossible to list particular rules for achieving balance through color. Some designers use scientific studies about color and others simply use a trained and intuitive eye. Here are some thinking processes to try:

• Complementary colors are opposites on the geometric color wheel and therefore seem to have the inherent ability to balance one another.

• The use of cool and warm hues, a method used by Paul Cézanne, can maintain a balance in the translation of light and shadow. Either the light stays warm and the shadows cool or vice versa.

• Bright hues or high chromas can be centrally located and surrounded by duller hues.

• Values can be controlled so that they stay within a close limited range.

• Color can be orchestrated, used at different points in the composition to move our eye from one point to another as well as to create a balance through distribution and placement.

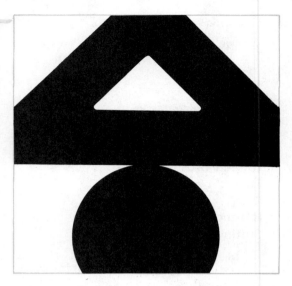

6-10a-b Student Work, *Retain Balance and Destroy Symmetry*
It is relatively simple to design a symmetrical image that is balanced. We merely counteract each form with its mirror image on each side of an imaginary vertical axis. In order to create a balanced asymmetrical image we must trust our intuitive sense of balance, as well as thinking about the inherent power of the page. Does the center have more power than the rest of the page? Can we place as much weight at the top of the page as at the bottom?

6-11a-b Student Work, *Retain Balance and Destroy Symmetry*
Always remember that there are innumerable solutions to a design problem. In the original symmetrical design the black shapes dominate the page. When we destroy the symmetry, the white of the page becomes much more active.

6-12a Student Work, *Retain Balance and Destroy Symmetry*
6-12b Nicolas Poussin, *The Birth of Venus*, 1638–40, oil on canvas
Courtesy of the Philadelphia Museum of Art, Philadelphia (The George W. Elkins Collection)
The simple geometric shapes of Figure 6-12a are balanced and symmetrical. The solution, Figure 6-12a, is similar to the composition by Poussin, *The Birth of Venus*. The segments of the circle in Figure 6-12a seem to float lyrically above the dispersed base the way the putti float in the sky in the composition by Poussin. The figures in each of the corners of the Poussin move diagonally toward the center focusing on the figure of Venus, whose birth is celebrated by the arch of drapery.

color orchestration

MATERIALS
- Illustration board
- Sketch pad
- H pencil
- Color-Aid pack
- Cutting tool
- Rubber cement

1. Design a balanced asymmetrical composition and then introduce color and maintain the balance.

2. Choose five low-chroma hues of different values and one high-chroma hue.

3. The low-chroma hues will physically dominate the space, but the bright hue will move our eye around the composition and create balance.

Knowledge Gained

We are forced to make initial decisions about hue, value, and chroma in our color choices. Then we must assess the different weights of the hues in order to maintain a balanced composition. Orchestrating a composition with a network of colors forces us to think of the total unit instead of thinking about color as separate from the design statement.

64

cool and warm

MATERIALS
- Illustration board
- Color-Aid pack
- Cutting tool
- Rubber cement

1. Choose 10 hues that are the same value.
2. Five hues must be cool and five must be warm. Although generally yellows, oranges, reds, and earth hues are warm and blues and greens are cool, any hue can be shifted by mixing inherently cool or warm hues into it.
3. Create a balanced composition by juxtaposing cool and warm hues.

Knowledge Gained
The ability to read value differences and cool and warm differences is perhaps the key to perceptual painting. Volume is determined by the accurate appraisal of these factors. Thinking and evaluating color in this way does not promote a reliance on a limited number of learned color harmonies, but fosters visual thinking.

**seven
focal point**

where are we supposed to look? what is the main point of the message/image?

The compositional design directs the viewer's eye within and around it, usually leading to the main focus of the work. Although we tend to be "center-oriented," thinking that the center of the page is where the focus must be, this is not always the case. In fact, artists from many eras have enjoyed moving the focus to unusual points in the container, even at times leaving us without a focus at all.

As Westerners trained by media such as theatre, film, and television, we are used to focusing on the center of things, rarely shifting our vision. In fact, in order to believe the illusion of a theatrical production or a television show, we must focus our vision away from the perimeters of the stage, screen, or set and place ourselves in the inner space of the ongoing illusion. The dominance of illusionism in film, television, and theatre in the Western world reinforces our sense of central focus.

There also seems to be a prejudice in favor of whole images. We were told in high school that a total image is a better image and that a centered well-balanced image is best for the sake of communication and clarity. Unfortunately, this oversimplifies matters. It sets enormous limits on possibilities. On the other hand, we must not ignore people's need for focus and clarity because they are obviously compelled by it; in the world of advertising design the message must be clearly stated.

How can we establish the focal point of an image? What type of elements dominate a page and in what way?

Position: the center of a page is dynamic.

Size: a large element dominates among smaller elements.

Shape: a different shape dominates among like shapes.

Direction: a different direction dominates among like directions.

Lines: particular types of lines are dynamic in relation to particular containers.

Hue: a different hue dominates among similar hues.

Value: a different value dominates among like values.

Chroma: a bright chroma is dynamic among lower chromas.

Isolation: an element left by itself dominates (though it probably is not dynamic).

Clarity: a clearly defined element dominates among blurred elements.

Texture: a textured element dominates among plain elements.

All elements leading to one element: This is the most difficult to achieve because it requires an organic compositional sense or knowledge.

Can we get all the pictorial elements in a composition to lead our eye to a single point of focus?

7-1 Sandro Botticelli, *The Adoration of the Magi*, paint on wood
Courtesy of the National Gallery of Art, Washington, D.C. (Andrew Mellon Collection)
Botticelli organizes many figures and forms to lead to one point of focus. All the figures are directed to the center of the painting, where the Madonna and Christ child are located. The architecture directs our vision there as well.

perceptual exercise in focal point

MATERIALS
• Still life materials
• Pad
• Pencil

PART I

1. Set up a still life or environment where all forms lead to a single focal point.
2. Extract simple lines from the perceptual information that lead to a point of focus on the page.
3. Make sure that you utilize the entire container.

PART II

MATERIALS
• 10-inch-square white illustration board
• Markers
• Pencils
• Sketch pad

1. Draw 10 arrows on a 10-inch square that all lead to a single point of focus.
2. They may be straight, diagonal, curved, or varied.
3. Do 10 thumbnail sketches and choose the one that is the most unpredictable and successful.

Knowledge Gained

As designers, we must learn to see the world with a trained eye. We cannot afford to be object oriented or literal. We must learn to see connections among objects, as well as underlying rhythms and forces. If we look at a city street we can begin to see how the curves of the street lights parallel one another. We can also see that people's gestures repeat architectural elements or forms in nature. For example, the curve of a leash made by someone walking a dog may repeat the curve of a sign or counter the curve of a light post.

7-2 Student Work, *Conceptual Exercise in Focal Point*

We must learn to look closely at our environment and extract meaning from it. Whether we want to impose order on what seems to be chaotic, reflect disorder, or reveal inherent order, we must look for repetitions, rhythms, connections, and focal points, or we must realize the absence of these qualities.

MULTIPLE POINTS OF FOCUS

How can we achieve more than one point of focus in one composition? Parallelism. Multiple focal points are alien to the way we see in a given moment. Biologically, we can focus only on one point at a time. Both our eyes operate to achieve one clear point in our field of vision. But by refocusing our vision we can take in a good deal more information. Therefore, one point of focus in a painting is accurate if we are thinking of a fixed point of view, but multiple focal points are accurate if we wish to communicate a field of information. Narrative and iconographic paintings as well as advertisements generally need multiple points of focus.

Although our eyes are capable of focusing on only one point at a time, we have become used to artificial mediums such as painting, photography, and advertising design that utilize multiple points of focus. All of these mediums produce concrete, fixed images. We may view these images in any order and in various ways. We can scan them, examine each part closely, or stand back to see the work in a glance, finding the main focus. Some paintings, such as Campin's *Merode Altarpiece*, are meant to be viewed from a close position. We are forced to view every object individually because of the amount of detail and solidity endowed to them by Campin. Or in the case of Hans Hofmann's work, *Memoria in Aeternum*, we move from one point of high chroma to another, shifting our position in space in response to each chromatic intensity. The lens of the camera allows us to see everything clearly in a split second, and at times we confuse photographic responses with our own. The photograph seems more real than our vision because everything is treated equally in detail, color, and volume. At times people comment that a particular painting has merit by saying, "It's so real it looks like a photograph!" This reaction is, of course, conditioned by a society dominated by technological or photographic images. People do not stop to think of the inherent differences between a camera's vision and human vision.

Advertising employs multiple focal points to communicate information. An advertisement may catch our eye with an effective graphic design or photograph which communicates the main part of the message. But the advertisers want us to read the supporting information as well. How

7-3 Robert Campin, *Merode Altarpiece*, fifteenth Century, oil on wood
Courtesy of the Metropolitan Museum of Art, New York (The Cloisters Collection)
All the forms in this tryptich are treated with equal care and detail, as if we were viewing all the forms from the same close distance. We understand that the artist was continuously refocusing his vision in order to see such detail.

does a good advertisement or painting motivate us to read everything in the composition? The answer lies in the creation of an organic composition, which in some way finds repetitions or parallels, counterpoints, rhythms, and connections between elements. The use of parallelism implies a sense of relatedness within the container. We understand that in order to get the main point we must investigate the other elements. We unconsciously assimilate the arrangement and read its information.

We are creators of systems, analogies, and harmonies; we look for order and we understand structures. We dance, make music, and write prose and poetry, and all these forms depend upon connections, parallels, and counterpoints. Design is a rational system that helps us read messages and meanings.

7-4 CBS Records, *Chicago*
John Berg, designer & art director,
Gerary Huerta, artist
All the curving lines of this "thumbprint" design lead our eye to the word *Chicago.*

7-5 (above) Giotto, *Lamentation,* fourteenth century, fresco
Courtesy of Arena Chapel, Padua, Italy
All the figures are focused on the figure of Christ. The figure with her back to us includes us in the concentrated focus of the moment. The diagonal wall leads us directly to Christ's head.

7-6 Piero della Francesca, *Resurrection,* fresco
Courtesy of Sansepolcro Town Hall, Italy
We focus on the vertical figure of Christ which forms the center axis. The trees in the background and the staff repeat the figure's verticality.

72

7-7 Jacopo Pontormo, *The Holy Family*, 1525,
oil on wood

Courtesy of the National Gallery of Art, Washington, D.C. (Samuel
H. Kress Collection)

Although the bottom figure of St. John points us to
the Christ child, we are meant to focus on the other
figures as well. Pontormo is able to achieve such
multiple points of focus by conceiving the five
figures as a unit with rhythmical curves as opposed
to thinking of them as separate objects.

73

7-8 Robin Landa, *Objects of Desire: Swan*, 1981,
oil on canvas
Courtesy of the Aaron Berman Gallery, New York
The drapery forms an inscribed circular unit
that brings our eye to each of the forms.
Each form is as clearly defined as the next. We
can focus on each form separately, but the swan
in the center attracts the eye because of
its central location.

analytical looking

MATERIALS
- Sketch pad
- Pencil

1. Choose an Old Master painting that has more than one point of focus and draw the underlying structure that organizes these focal points.

2. Choose an advertisement that sets up parallels between elements. Draw the underlying structure.

Knowledge Gained

A designer must have the ability to structure elements so that they communicate. Reading the skeletal structures of other artists' works enlarges our range and provokes analytical looking.

7-9a Edgar Degas, *Ballet Scene*, pastel
Courtesy of the National Gallery of Art, Washington, D.C. (Chester Dale Collection)
The gesture of one dancer leads us to the gesture of the next dances across the space.

7-9b Student Work, *Analytical Looking*
As designers, we must learn to analyze the underlying structures of fine art and commercial art, so that we may learn from them.

75

color as a focal point

MATERIALS
- Tempera paints (black, white, red, yellow, blue, green)
- 10-inch-square white illustration board
- Brush
- H pencil
- Ruler

1. Rule the board into a 1-inch-square grid with the H pencil.

2. Following the diagram, first place the bright hues—red, yellow, blue, and green—in their appropriate boxes.

3. All mixed colors in a given line should match the value of the high-chroma hue that begins the line. Begin with Roman numeral I and be sure to move in numerical order. Begin by mixing the formula of the innermost box on a line. After the first mixture of the high-chroma hue with black and white keep mixing all following steps into the original mixture, constantly adjusting the values.

5. Adjust all values with white at all times to lighten.

6. The open boxes may be individually filled with any mixture. Make sure that the color choices in these areas do not conflict with the established points of high chroma and that they do make coloristic connections to the six lines.

Knowledge Gained

This project is designed to give a good deal of palette experience in a short time. It teaches us to read the value of a bright hue and maintain a value line. We learn to create subtle variations within hues and realize the innumerable number of grays that can be mixed from colors. If just red, yellow, blue, black, and white yield so many grays, imagine the possibilities as we extend the palette to include all the other hues. Most importantly, we have experienced high-chroma colors as focal points in a low-chroma field. The open boxes force us to think about the total container as one color statement. We must work to establish parallels and connections among the four areas and the six lines.

7-10 (facing page) Diagram for Project 7.3, *Color as Focal Point*

				VII	I				
				Red + Yellow + Black + Green 4	Red + Yellow + Black 4				
				Red + Blue + Green 3	Red + Blue 3				
		B		Red + Yellow + Green 2	Red + Yellow 2		Y		
				Red + Black + White + Green 1	Red + Black + White 1				
Green + Blue + Black 4	Green + Yellow 3	Green + Red 2	Green + Black + White 1	G	R	Blue + Black + White + Red 1	Blue + Red + Red 2	Blue + Yellow + Red 3	Blue + Yellow + Red + Red 4
Green + Blue + Black + Yellow 4	Green + Blue + Yellow 3	Green + Red + Yellow 2	Green + Black + White + Yellow 1	Y	B	Blue + Black + White 1	Blue + Red 2	Blue + Yellow 3	Blue + yellow + Red 4
		R		Yellow + Black + White + 1	Yellow + Black + White + Blue 1		G		
				Yellow + Red 2	Yellow + Red + Blue 2				
				Yellow + Blue 3	Yellow + Blue + Blue 3				
				Yellow + Green 4	Yellow + Blue + Green 4				
				II	VI				

IV V

VIII III

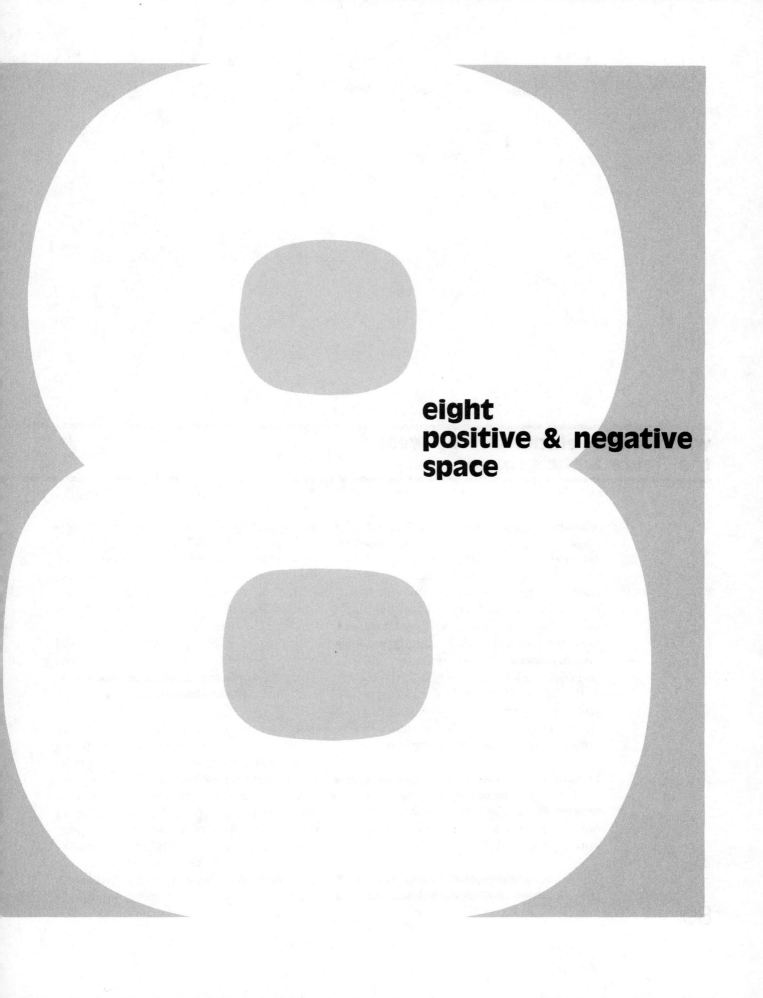

eight
positive & negative
space

what is the relationship between the figure & the ground?

The artist has a responsibility to the blank page. The page, which we call the *container,* is a given element made up of two verticals and two horizontals that is immediately made active by any added element. Once a mark is made on the blank page it becomes the *figure* or *positive space* and the page becomes the *ground* or *negative space*. A poor designer will not consider the leftover space, only the figure. A thoughtful designer will always see the page as a constantly active force that shares importance with the direct mark, which is the figure or positive space.

Becoming conscious of the negative space makes you design the total unit as one organic field. The positive space or figure has much more force and power when the entire page is fully considered.

There are instances in design when both the positive and negative spaces are equally active. An ideal example of this is the Chinese *yin-yang* symbol. This symbol represents *yang*, which is considered to be the masculine element (light), and *yin*, which is thought to be the feminine (dark). The circle, being a perfect shape, is made up of both these elements; both *yin* and *yang* complement each other and create perfect balance and harmony. There is no figure and no ground, since both are equally dynamic shapes.

Although this use of positive and negative or figure/ground space is perfect in the sense that the figure/ground can reverse, its absolute equality and identical nature of form enhance visual abstraction. It is necessary to experience this relationship of forms through a process-oriented experiment in order to assimilate a sense of positive and negative space and to answer the question: "What is the relationship between the figure and the ground?"

80

8-1 If we are object oriented and see the figure as the only important design element, we are not using the total design medium. We have a responsibility to design the entire space, even the "empty space."

8-2 *Yin-Yang*
This oriental symbol utilizes the theory of positive and negative space. Both the black shape and the white shape are equally important. Both shapes can act as the Figure and as the ground.

81

what is the figure?
what is the ground?

MATERIALS
- Black and white tempera paint
- 10-inch-square *gray* illustration board
- Brush

1. On a 10-inch-square gray illustration board create a black curvilinear shape within the square that engages the energies of the four sides.

Result: Black direct mark on gray container.

2. Paint a white X or cross through the black shape. The X should cross all borders.
Result: White mark on black shape.

3. With white paint, paint the rest of the board so that it connects up with the X. This should create four pielike shapes with no ground color left. Can you now define the figure and ground priorities? Do the black shapes float in the white field or does the white X seem to be in front of a black space?

Knowledge Gained
In step 1 the black curvilinear shape was the figure on a gray ground. In step 2 a figure, the white X, was placed over the original figure, making it the ground. In step 3 the original gray ground was covered over and destroyed by the white paint. Depending upon how well you engaged the energies of the container, the four black shapes and the white X should be seen both as figure and as ground. This flip/flop of forms is dependent upon the way the viewer focuses on the respective images.

Now that this concept is internalized we can use recognizable shapes to create dynamic positive/negative relationships. The use of type and the art of typography is pervasive in commercial art today. If type is not well designed spatially it does not work—it does not read. The designer must completely understand the leftover spaces of the letter forms and the page.

8-3a-c Diagram of the process for *What is the Figure? What is the Ground?* In step 1, the black curvilinear shape is the figure on a gray ground. In step 2 a figure, the white X, is placed over the original figure, making the black curvilinear shape the ground. In step 3 the original gray ground is covered over and destroyed by the white paint.

(a)

(b)

(c)

8-4 Student Work, *What is the Figure? What is the Ground?*
We should be able to flip/flop our vision between the black shapes and the white X. The black shapes should activate the entire space. They should be strategically positioned.

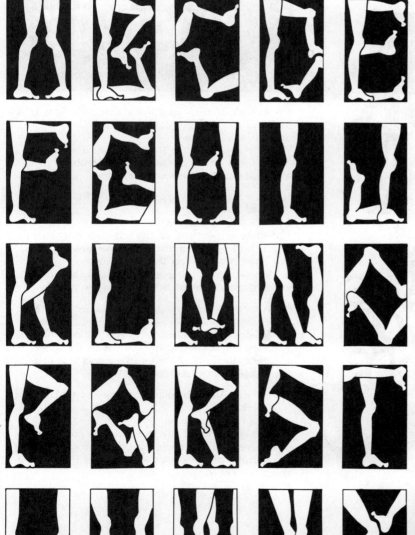

8-5 Mary Ann Smith, designer, New York, *Knee Caps*, alphabet
Each letter of the alphabet is conceived in relation to its own container, and the black space is as active as the letters formed by the legs.

83

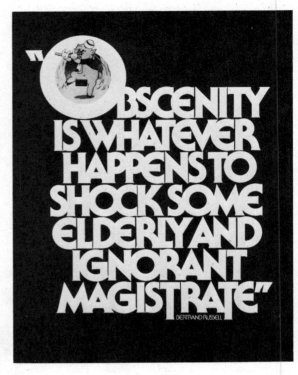

8-6 Alan Peckolick, typographic designer, New York
Dansk, logo
Lubalin Peckolick Associates
The overlapping of the letters creates a pattern
that connects them as an inseparable unit.
A logo should be read as a tight unit.

8-7 Alan Peckolick, typographic designer, New York
One Trick Pony, logo
© Lubalin Peckolick Associates
The space in between all the letters is extremely
active. Notice the white triangles formed by the
two letter *N*'s. We can feel a continuous
rhythm set up as our eyes move from the first *O*
to the *C* and then to the *O* in *Pony*.

8-8 Alan Peckolick, typographic designer, New York
The Bedside Book of Bastards
© Lubalin Peckolick Associates
The continuous curving movements in the letters
are arabesquelike and connect the words to read as
a unit rather than as separate words.

8-9 (above) Alan Peckolick, typographic designer,
New York
© Lubalin Peckolick Associates
The eleven words in this quote act as one unit,
where every space between every letter and word is
thoughtfully designed. A good designer thinks
about the entire space.

84

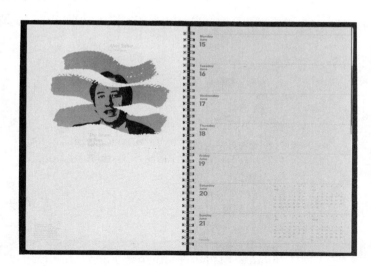

8-10 Champion International Corporation,
Champions of the Future, appointment calendar, 1981
Bruce Blackburn, design director,
Danne & Blackburn, Inc., New York
At times the white painterly marks of the page
seem to move in front of the black and grey image.
If we focus on the image, then the white marks
move behind the image.

8-11 (right, top) Barbara Dodsworth,
calligrapher, New York
The beauty of calligraphic letter forms is enhanced
by the deliberate consideration of positive and
negative space. The bottoms of the top row of
letters seem to answer the movements of the top of
the letters beneath them.

8-12 (second from top) Barbara Dodsworth,
calligrapher, New York
Although the bottom left corner is untouched by
line, the space takes on a shape caused by the
curving lines of the positive letter forms.

8-13 (third from top) Barbara Dodsworth,
calligrapher, New York
This calligraphic alphabet creates interesting
shapes when the letters are juxtaposed to one
another and to a tight container.

8-14 (bottom, right) Barbara Dodsworth,
calligrapher, New York
This lower-case *n* seems to sit on the cropped Form
of another *n*. The white space in the center of
the *n* can come forward if we focus on it.

85

letter forms

MATERIALS

- Black and white tempera paint
- 10-inch-square white illustration board
- Brush
- Pencil
- Sketch pad
- Type catalog

PART I

1. Using your initials, work out a design on the board that will read as easily in terms of black on white as white on black. You are designing not only the letters themselves, but, in effect, also the space they leave.

2. The letters must at some point touch all four sides of the square.

3. You may use any kind of typeface.

4. You may also crop the letters or reverse them.

Example: Using the letters *R* and *L*, design the space the letters leave over as carefully as the letter forms themselves. The forms can be read as an *R* and *L* or as rectangles, triangles, and curved free forms. (See facing page.)

PART II

MATERIALS

- Black and white tempera paint
- Four 10-inch-square illustration boards
- Pencil
- Sketch pad
- Brushes

1. On four 10-inch-squares set up a sequence of letter forms. Each container should work separately while still coordinating and working as a unit in a combined horizontal format.

2. The first square may be your previous project utilizing your initials, or you may choose two other letters. The second square should have 4 letters, the next 8 letters, and the last square 16 letters. (See pp. 88-89.)

3. As in Part I the letters must at some point touch all four sides of the container. The negative space of the letter forms must be active shapes. The field must read in both its positive space and its negative space.

Note: A vocabulary of form will have been set up in the first square by virtue of your choice of typeface. That is, you will have chosen to use straight letters or curved letters, letters with serifs or sans-serif letters. This vocabulary of form must be continued in all four squares; it is necessary in order to effect a flow from one unit to the next. Notice that the number of letters doubles from one square to the next; this will cause a decrease in the scale of the letters from panel to panel. You may wish to emphasize this scale change; if not, you may choose to imply one letter in another, thereby having fewer forms to occupy the same space. For example, an *n* is implied in an *h*, a *P* in an *R*.

8-15 Diagram *Letter Forms*
The *R* and *L* can be read as letters or as
rectangles, triangles, and curved free forms. When
we design letters, we must think of the space
left over by the letters as active.

8-16 Student Work, *Letter Forms*
The letter *N* is inscribed in the letter *S*
to form powerful negative shapes. The entire
square is activated.

8-17 Student Work, *Letter Forms*
We can read this design as either four triangles
or as an *S* and an *N*.

8-18a-d Student Work, *Extended Letter Forms*
The *K* and *F* in the first panel are directly linked to the edge of
the second panel. Although the letter forms in this solution are much
more readable than the lettes in Figure 8.17, the open space
is no less powerful. Each panel leads to the next and there
are diagonals, verticals, and horizontals that set up rhythmical
repeats and counterpoints. The artist tied up the edges of the
last panel and set a diagonal in the upper-right-hand corner that
redirects our eyes back to the third panel.

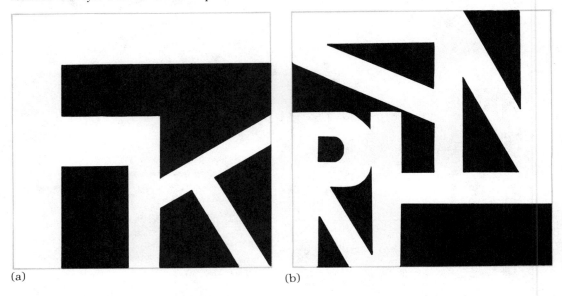

(a)   (b)

8-19a-d Student Work, *Extended Letter Forms*
This artist did a wonderful job of alternating the ground
and letters win terms of black and white in the last three panels.
The *R* and the *I* in the first panel are in white; in the second
panel the *M* and *E* are in black and the linked *J* and *K* are
in white. The scale takes a radical drop from the first panel with
2 letters to the last panel with 16 letters. Our eyes are able
to maintain a flow across the panels because similar movements are
established in all the panels.

(a)   (b)

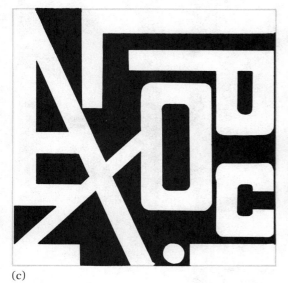

(c)

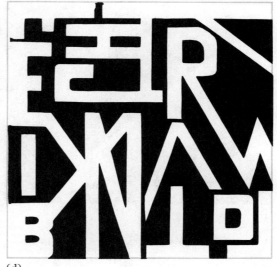

(d)

(c)

(d)

89

8-20a-d Student Work, *Extended Letter Forms*
The angular *S* and *J* in the first panel immediately set
up a vocabulary of internal triangles and geometrics that is
kept up throughout the four panels. There is an excellent movement
back and forth in these four panels between black and white.

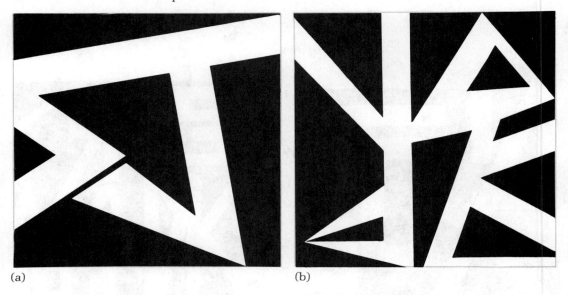

(a)   (b)

8-21a-d Student Work, *Extended Letter Forms*

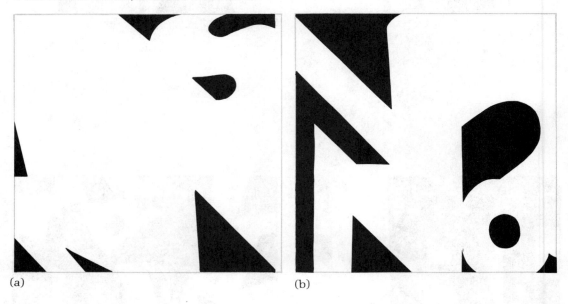

(a)   (b)

(c)

(d)

(c)

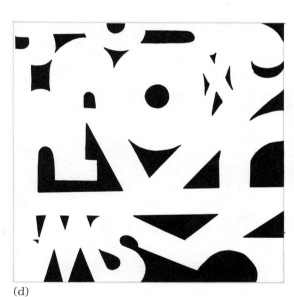

(d)

91

Knowledge Gained

We have learned to see all space as active. In fact, the negative space can at times overpower the positive. We have learned to maintain a vocabulary of forms through an extended field, and have had a container stand alone as well as be part of a larger whole. We have gained the ability to change the scale of forms within a constant container size.

The concept of positive/negative space is the most important element of design. Whether the designer paints paintings, designs advertisements or album covers, or does layouts, the understanding that there is no such thing as "leftover" space and that "no space is ever background or unused" will undoubtedly lead to dynamic composition. This does not mean that if there is any blank space it must be filled with clutter or meaningless forms, but rather that the artist must constantly be aware of the spaces the figure makes with the page. Open space can be dynamic depending upon the positive elements.

8-22 Édouard Manet, *The Dead Toreador*, oil on canvas
Courtesy of the National Gallery of Art, Washington, D.C.
(Widener Collection)
Manet gives us little more than the figure and cloth on the ground to indicate a ground plane. There is no subdivision to indicate a separation between the floor and wall. But the space is tense and we are convinced that there is a floor plane in spite of the lack of details and the depth of the shadow.

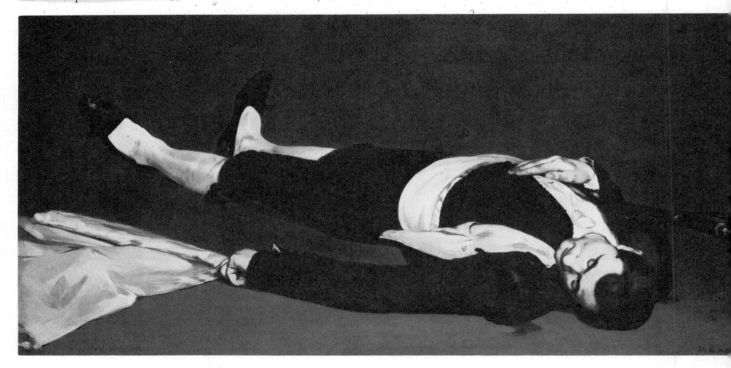

8-23 Edgar Degas, *Carriage at the Races*,
oil on canvas

Courtesy of the Museum of Fine Arts, Boston
(Purchased, Arthur Gordon Tompkins Risiduary Fund)

Although there is a great deal of open space,
the positioning of the positive elements
creates tension and activates the entire surface
in this work.

93

active open space

MATERIALS
- Black and white tempera paint
- 10-inch-square white illustration board
- Brush

1. Using your initials, create an active figure/ground design.

2. The letters may only touch two sides of the square container. They may touch two adjacent sides *or* two opposite sides.

Note: It is recommended that many small thumbnail sketches be done before deciding on the final design. You may ultimately choose your first idea, but this will allow more possibilities to occur.

Knowledge Gained

We understand that "empty" space can be active. The dynamics of the untouched space are dependent upon the shape of the container and, of course, on how the direct marks respond to and use the untouched space.

8-24 Student Work, *Active Open Space*
The positioning of the B in relation to the vast amount of white space truly engages the open area. The two half-circles of the B push toward the open area.

8-25 Student Work, Active Open Space

the common object

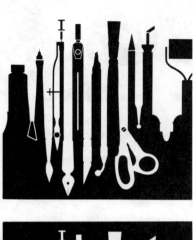

8-26a-b Academy of Art College, San Francisco; at top is opened inside spread for the semester program
Henry Brimmer, designer-Instructor, San Francisco
Both the black and white shapes are art tools. Mr. Brimmer almost touches the bottom and top edges, constantly moving our eyes up and down the beautifully shaped spaces.

8-27 A.I. Friedman, Inc. *A.I. Friedman*, catalog cover
Tobias Moss, art director, New York, and
Hans Allemann, graphic artist, New York
These common art tools are made very exciting by their placement in the container and their interaction with the white space.

95

MATERIALS
- Black and white tempera paint
- White illustration board
- Pencil
- Brush
- Objects

1. Using a common object such as a paper clip, scissors, a hammer, or a keychain, create a figure/ground design.

2. The object may retain recognizability, but the negative space must be active. You may change the scale and direction of the object. The shapes may also overlap.

Knowledge Gained

It seems that we are trained to be "object oriented" in this society. Once the element of recognizability is introduced, we tend to forget all learned abstract concepts. This project allows us to design objects, always keeping in mind the abstract concept of positive/negative space. It is this abstraction of dynamic imagery that gives objects force on a page.

8-28 Student Work, *The Common Object*
The change in scale of the insect increases the dynamics. The edges play an important role in the cropping of the forms to create an interesting pattern.

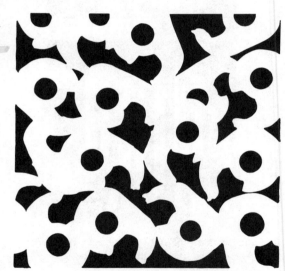

8-29 Student Work, *The Common Object*
This design was created by simply tracing the tape dispenser in different overlapping positions. The circles and free-form shapes can appear to be black figures on a white ground.

cropped imagery

MATERIALS
- Black and white tempera paint
- 20-by-24-inch white illustration board
- Brushes

1. Using perceptual information such as trees, branches, insects, plants, and flowers, create a figure/ground design that closes in and at some points or all points crops the imagery.

Knowledge Gained

Cropped imagery or closeups force us to exercise a certain aspect of our vision. We use our sense of sight in many different ways; we can take in a whole field of many objects and forms or from the same distance force our eyes to zoom in on a particular form. This exercise forces us to pull one item out of the environment; we must visually focus with an intention in mind. We will also be enlarging the scale from the size of the previous containers used. This increase in scale will lend force to our zoom vision.

Positive/negative space or figure/ground design should not only be thought of in relation to modern art, television, film, or commercial art. It was a concept that the Old Masters utilized in their representational paintings. Their use of it is simply quieter and acts as part of the underlying compositional structure. It does not scream for our attention as it does in twentieth-century art, but nevertheless, it operates on the same guiding principle. It acts underneath the story level, on the level of good composition in the skeleton of the picture.

Television today makes extensive use of figure/ground design. The Pepsi-Cola Company makes effective use of this technique in its current advertising campaign for brand Diet Pepsi, themed "Now You See It, Now You Don't." (See plate 00.) All visuals used in this print and television campaign make use of cropped images. It is an extraordinarily effective visual treatment. It uses closeup shots, and even though all figures and objects are cut off or cropped in some way, we still recognize them. This visual sophistication on the part of the viewing public has probably been nurtured by photography and zoom lenses, television and movie closeups. The original influence was probably fine art, which commercial art quickly adopted

8-30 Student Work, *Cropped Imagery*
This design of a drain pipe is broken into simple shapes that take up the entire space of the small container; the pipe visually enlarges the container.

with large billboards and magazine advertisements. The viewing public constantly demands innovative methods of seeing; it needs to be visually excited. Cropped imagery is an undeniably powerful tool. With graphic impact, it establishes immediate intimacy.

8-31 Barbara Dodsworth calligrapher, New York
Letters can be cropped and still be readable.

8-32 City Center, *Contemporary Ballet*, NYC, 1980, poster
Robert Mapplethorpe, photographer, Lake End Graphics Ltd.
Cropped imagery brings us very close to the subject matter and
feel much more intimate with the forms. Mr. Mapplethorpe's
photographs allow us to see the imagery both as identifiable forms
and as exciting shapes.

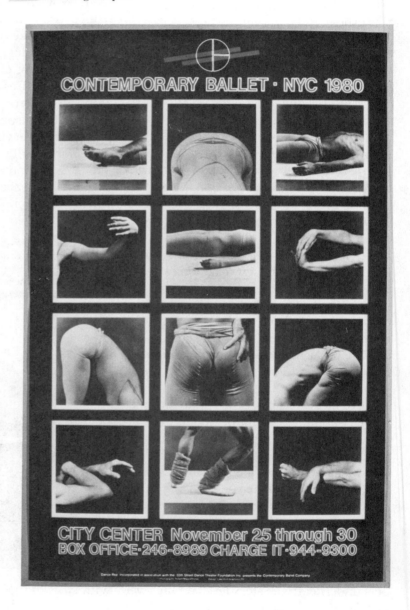

8-33 PepsiCo Diet Pepsi, *Urban* (advertising campaign)
Reprinted with permission of © PepsiCo, Inc., 1981.

BBDO
Batten, Barton, Durstine & Osborn, Inc.

Client	PEPSI-COLA		Time	30 SECONDS
Product:	DIET PEPSI	Title: "URBAN"	Comml. No.	PEDX-0103

SINGERS: Now you see it

Now you don't.

Here you have it

Here you won't.

Diet Pepsi one small calorie

Now you see it

Now you don't.

That great Pepsi taste

Diet Pepsi

won't go to your waist.

Now you see it

Now you don't.

Diet Pepsi one small calorie

Now you see it...

Now you don't.

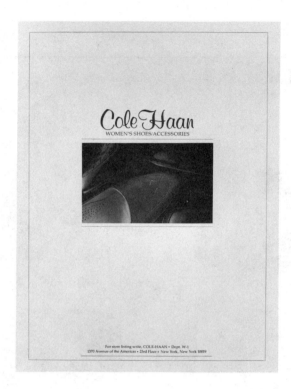

8-34 Cole-Haan, *Cole-Haan*, magazine advertisement
The use of cropped imagery in advertising is popular and effective. We get to see the product up close and we look at it as a form, a thing of beauty, instead of as an object.

the old masters

MATERIALS
- Black and white tempera paint
- A reproduction of an Old Master painting
- Illustration board scaled to the size of the print
- Brushes
- Pencil

1. Choose a reproduction (a black and white reproduction is easier) of a painting by one of the following artists: Vermeer (Dutch, seventeenth century); Caravaggio (Italian, seventeenth century); Poussin (French, seventeenth century); Piero della Francesca (Italian, fifteenth century); or Edward Hopper (American, twentieth century).

2. Break the areas into black, gray, and white shapes. Do not be too concerned with details, just major forms.

Knowledge Gained

We will begin to realize the importance of figure/ground design to good composition. Whether we are dealing in pure abstraction or representation, the underlying principles are the same. All space must be considered active and alive.

Just as the principle of positive/negative space acts to engage the viewer's eye and enhance or communicate meaning, so does color. Many scientists and scholars believe that we make color choices on a deeper level than "taste." Therefore, color has the ability to affect the viewer. Some artists in the nineteenth century believed deeply in the psychological effects of color—for example, Van Gogh, Seurat, Signac, and Gauguin. In the Renaissance color held religious meanings; certain colors were associated with the Virgin Mary and other biblical figures. Color symbolism was dependent upon the church and the particular geographic location.

One of the most popular harmonies the public utilizes is *analogous harmony* or *adjacent hues. Analogous* could be interpreted as meaning "belonging to" or "paralleling," as in one family. For example, while sisters might not be identical twins, there is often a family likeness. It literally refers to hues that are positioned next to each other or adjacent on the geometric color wheel. *Harmony* indicates an inherent agreement or cooperation of the hues. It is also a result of "how" you pick the adjacent hues in relative value and chroma. The range of hue variation should be limited to a narrow pie-wedge section of the geometric color wheel (such as blue-violet through blue-green or yellow-orange through orange-red) so that the family resemblance is maintained about a dominant hue.

Pages 102 and 103:

8-35 Jan Vermeer, *Young Woman with a Water Jug,* oil on canvas
Courtesy of the Metropolitan Museum of Art, New York, (Gift of Henry G. Marquand)
Vermeer carefully composed this painting, endowing every shape with energy. The figure and objects break the rear wall into separate and energetic shapes.

8-36 Jan Vermeer, *Woman Holding a Balance,* 1664, oil on canvas
Courtesy of the National Gallery of Art, Washington D.C. (Widener Collection)

analogous harmony

MATERIALS
- Color-Aid pack
- 11-by-14-inch gray illustration board
- Cutting tool
- Rubber cement
- Pencil
- Sketch pad

1. Choose a pie wedge of adjacent hues from the geometric color wheel. The amount or degree of variation in hue is up to you—for instance, you may choose very close hues (YO, YOO, O, OOR, and OR) or a wider range (YOY, OY, O, OR, and ROR). In both cases orange is the predominant hue. *There should be a predominance of one hue.* The predominant hue may be primary, secondary, or compound.

2. Choose all the hues in different values and chromas that fall into a particular wedge area out of the pack.

3. Select out a minimum of five hues, always remembering that one hue should dominate the color statement, and an unlimited number of hues within the section of the wheel. That is, there may be four hues between YO and YOO, besides O, OOR, and OR. Use as many variations of value and chroma of each of the hues selected as desired.

4. The ultimate selection of the range in value and chroma along with the visual ambiance of one hue will result in a unique color statement.

5. *The Design:* Instead of the conventional usage of a rectangular container, we will be using a *tondo* or round container. It seems fitting in relation to the theory's derivation from the geometric color wheel as well as to the inherent flowing nature of analogous harmony. Analogous harmony tends to make a lyrical color statement because the colors are adjacent to one another and therefore have a natural association. Logically, design should enhance the color theory. Our aim is to move with the flow of the circular container, keeping its closure firm both literally and figuratively, and never breaking the actual boundary.

8-37 Student Work
Shapes can be designed in terms of positive/negative space within a tondo to create volume and movement. The curving shapes of the artist's initials in this work give the effect of convex volume. They move with the tondo and do not break the flow.

6. Do a number of thumbnail sketches before choosing the final design. Keep in mind the design properties of curved shapes and lines, as well as those of straight shapes and lines. Remember that all elements inside the tondo will be reacting to a powerful circular border. First design impulses can be clichéd in response to achieving a flowing solution; pushing our resources allow us to come up with atypical answers to harmonious design. Allow the particular qualities of the selected hues, values, and chromas to influence the mode and mood of the design solution.

7. Execute the final design in a tondo 10 inches in diameter, mounting it on a gray illustration board. A medium-valued gray will enhance the color solution. Why is that so?

Knowledge Gained

We have learned to discriminate between small hue variations, such as the difference between YO and YOO. We can only understand these minute hue differences by placing colors next to one another for comparison. Through a limitation process, selecting only certain values and chromas, we have created a color statement, producing a color effect. Combining a harmonious theory of color with design theory has strengthened our understanding of art as a cohesive medium.

Analogous harmony is a very popular theory in fashion, advertising, and interior design because of its inherent consonance. It has a tonic and pleasing quality. This may be due to the fact that the colors are adjacent, neighbors in a sense.

We have previously explored the nature of complementary colors. Complements can enhance or nullify one another, depending upon their scale, value, and placement. They set up vibration and excitement. Let us take a further look at their potential.

8-38 Student Work

8-39 Student Work
When we think of figure/ground design we usually mean the design of shapes rather than of line. But line can divide the space into shapes.

If you take a pair of complements on the geometric color wheel and replace one of the complementary colors with adjacent hues on either side of it you form an inscribed isosceles triangle. A *tetrad* is made up of two pairs of complements or by inscribing a square or rectangle. A *hexad* is made up of three pairs of complements or two pairs of complements plus black and white.

Each of these color groupings can express a color harmony, as we have explored in analogous harmony, but here there can also be dissonance or tension.

105

split complement

MATERIALS
- Color-Aid pack
- 11-by-14-inch gray illustration board
- Cutting tool
- Rubber cement
- Pencil
- Sketch pad

1. Choose a pair of complements from the geometric color wheel; they may be singular or compound hues. Then replace one end of the pair with its adjacent hues— that is, split one end. For example, you may choose red and green and then replace green with blue-green and yellow-green (R + G into R + BG + YG), or choose yellow-orange and blue-violet and replace blue-violet with blue and violet (YO + BV into YO + B + V).

2. Limit the number of hues to the three that comprise the split complement. Choose any number of values and chromas of these three hues. Since this theory is inherently dissonant, choose values and chromas that will add to the dissonance and tension.

3. *The Design:* Once again we will use a tondo as the container. But this time we will try to create tension in the circular container. Our aim is to break the flow of the tondo without physically moving outside the circular border, thereby adding to the colors' discord.

4. Do many thumbnail sketches before making a final design decision.

Knowledge Gained

Although the complements in this project are indirectly opposed, they maintain their inherent reaction to one another. All of this may seem quite scientifically oriented and overwhelming, but it is very important to remember that above all else color emanates feelings and meanings. Many theoreticians throughout history, such as Goethe, Henry, and Rood, have opinions on the particular feelings each color gives off and whether or not these feelings are part of a universal language. But nevertheless, the point to be remembered is that color can be made to be very communicative and special. If we juxtapose two opposite theories, such as analogous harmony and split complement, and design them in the same type of container, their dynamic differences will be revealed.

Much of modern abstract painting has been about the attempt to solve the problem of locating color in space. Painters more or less divorced themselves from figuration and concentrated on color interaction. Hans Hofmann was concerned with the "push and pull" of color in space, and other painters such as Rothko and Albers related color to design forms. This concept is a sophisticated one since it demands the ability to read color weights. The weight of a color is determined by its value, chroma, and relative opacity.

8-40 (facing page) Wohl Shoe Company, *Marquise* (a federally registered trademark of Wohl Shoe Company, St. Louis, Missouri.) In this ad, the angles of the footwear are extremely dynamic because they are set in a tondo. The arches are basically vertical and the horizontal ground plane pressures the tondo container.

8-41 Raphael, *Madonna and Child with the Infant St. John*, oil

Galleria Palatina Palazzo Pitti Maseuss, Florence, Italy

The only vertical in this painting is the arm of the chair. This vertical defines the position of figures in space. If we take out the vertical arm of the chair, the figures seem to float in space. The Madonna, child and St. John are rounded and move with the flow of the container. The tondo is an embrace of the loving subject of mother and son.

8-42 Arshile Gorky, *Image in Xhorkum*, 1936, oil

Courtesy of the Sidney Janis Gallery, New York

The forms that Gorky paints are clearly dependent upon one another for their position in space and their respective edges. The forms flip/flop back and forth for a forward position in space. They tie up the surface and at no point in the work do we move far back into space.

8-43 Mary Cassatt, *The Boating Party*, 1893-94, oil on canvas
Courtesy of the National Gallery of Art, Washington, D.C.
(Chester Dale Collection)

The point of view is clearly established by the male figure in the right-hand corner. If we stand to the right of the painting the space opens up diagonally toward the upper-left-hand corner, but the space tends to move up rather than back. This move up the surface is caused by the extremely high horizon line and the fact that both the negative and positive shapes are interesting and active. Notice that the water is broken into shapes by the positive forms. The diagonal line of the oar, which creates a slight amount of depth, is stopped and linked to the form of the bottom edge of the boat, which makes a shape with the water.

8-44 Franz Kline, *Lehigh v. Span*, 1960, oil on canvas
Courtesy of the Sidney Janis Gallery, New York
We understand the black brush marks to be the direct, positive marks and yet the white spaces come forward strongly. The entire surface of the canvas is engaged by the black strokes.

8-45 The Broadway, Los Angeles, California, *The Broadway*, (magazine advertisement as seen in *Vogue*, November 1981).
This ad incorporates the use of photography and black and white figure/ground design. The dynamic shapes made by the shadow of the figure lead us to the figure, which is the focal point.

color &
positive/negative space

MATERIALS
• Color-Aid pack or paints
• 4 10-inch-square illustration boards
• Project 8-2

1. Utilizing our Extended Letter Forms project, translate the black and white shapes into color. Set up color interactions by juxtaposing different weights of color against one another, constantly thinking about their position in space.

2. Vary the chromas, values, and opaque and translucent colors to make some colors advance and others recede. Remember that cool grayed colors tend to recede and warm bright colors advance.

3. The design will entail all four panels of the Extended Letter Forms project. A language of form has been established in Project 8-2, Part II, that moves the viewer's eye across all four surfaces. Now continue the concept of a flow across the surfaces by using the language of color.

Knowledge Gained
The understanding of where one color sits in space in relation to another color must be empirically derived. We have acquired the ability to manipulate, and to push and pull color, as well as to command a visual reading from one surface to another.

**nine
vertical &
horizontal
extensions**

what is the difference between a
regular rectangle & a prolonged rectangle?

Whether we wish to use the real world as a source for our designs or to ignore representational references, we can learn an enormous amount about the design process through an investigation of how we perceive reality and translate space. We accept the translation of the three-dimensional world onto a two-dimensional surface because we have grown up with a wonderful history of successful examples. In order to participate in the process of translating three dimensions into two, we must investigate the way we see. We must realize that particular formal design elements have the potential to communicate spatial relationships.

When we depict a three-dimensional environment on a two-dimensional surface, we have to make certain decisions about the type of space and spatial relationships we want to communicate to the viewer. Our distance from the image, our point of view, and the container we choose are decisions we must make in the design process. These decisions will communicate various types of vision or space.

SCALE

Our distance from the image is primarily communicated through scale. The size of the shapes in the design in relation to the size of the container will tell the viewer how close he or she is to the design. We assume that when images are large in scale they are close to us. For example, if an image is cropped or cut off, we assume that we are so close to it that we can only see part of it. When images are small in scale, we assume that they are at a distance from us.

ENTRY

A definite point of entry into a composition or design can communicate the position of the viewer in relation to the design.

Nicolas Poussin gives the viewer a definite point of entry into *The Rape of the Sabine Women*. This entry occurs across the ground plane; the painting is much more spacious if we stand to the left and follow this point of entry. Entry can be gained at any area in the space that deliberately opens up and brings our eye in.

POINT OF VIEW

The point of view tells the viewer whether the artist was to the right, to the left, or directly in front of the image. It also tells the viewer about the artist's eye level, whether he or she was above, below, or level with the image.

CONTAINER

Different containers are appropriate for different types of space. Squares and regular rectangles may be best for translating frontal images and regular space. On the other hand, extensions may be best for translating peripheral vision and elongated space.

In representational works, we usually compress space into a theaterlike or boxlike stage setting where there is some sense of floor and wall and at times a sense of the ceiling. The space we are translating onto the page is generally much much larger than the page, and we compress the imagery in order to achieve the translation from the three-dimensional world to the two-dimensional surface. We shift our eyes back and forth to include all the things seen into a regular rectangle. But what about communicating extended vision or peripheral vision instead of the more common compressed vision? How do we deal with it? How does the meaning shift when we shift specific types of containers?

extended vision

MATERIALS
- 18-by-24-inch newsprint pad
- Charcoal
- Kneaded eraser

PART I: VERTICAL VISION

1. Stand at a fixed point in a room with a drawing table at your right side if you are right-handed and at your left if you are left-handed, with your pad held vertically.
2. Begin drawing the space above you, looking up, and recording it with very general lines and shapes on the page.
3. Continue drawing and start shifting your vision downward.
4. Do not attempt to draw the full vertical span of the space on one page. Add pages as they are needed.
5. After drawing the entire vertical space, arrange the pages vertically on a flat surface. Notice all the spatial shifts and drops in your vision.
6. Repeat the process, but this time record all the information on one page. Compress the four or five pages into one vertical page.

PART II: HORIZONTAL VISION

1. Stand at a fixed point in a room with a drawing table in front of you and your pad held horizontally.
2. Begin drawing the space to the right of you. Do not move your entire body; move only your head. Add paper as needed.
3. Continue recording the room space in general lines and shapes, turning your head slowly to the left.
4. After drawing the entire horizontal span of your vision, arrange the four or five pages horizontally on a flat surface. Notice all the spatial connections and peculiarities.
5. Repeat the process, but this time record all the information on one page. Compress the four or five pages into one horizontal page.

Knowledge Gained

When we draw or record the vertical or horizontal span of our vision on several pages, we have plenty of room to express the distance our eyes travel. When we compress the span of vision into one vertical or horizontal extension, we can begin to understand just how much we do compress vision when we translate three dimensions into two. The use of extensions to express extended vision is clear; a regular rectangle suppresses the expression of extended vision.

Vertical and horizontal extensions are metaphors for types of extended vision, space, and meaning. A vertical extension, a vertically prolonged rectangle, has been used traditionally to represent divisions of heaven, earth, and hell, or sky, land, and water, especially during the Renaissance and Baroque eras. In the late nineteenth and early twentieth centuries, artists such as Vuillard, Bonnard, and Matisse used vertical and horizontal extensions to communicate their perceived fields of vision and visual peripheries. Extensions can be interpreted as a metaphor of unity. For instance, the continuity between inside space and outside space can be communicated through a continuous vertical field. Henri Matisse, a modern French painter, sees the visual world as retaining continuity. In his works *The Blue Window* and *The Piano Lesson* there is a sense of flow between in and out and up and down. These works are carefully organized to move our eyes slowly up rather than out of the space. Artists working representationally in the twentieth century could ally themselves with the modernist concept of maintaining the inherent flatness of the picture plane through the use of extensions. For example, even if a work is representational, verticals within the extended vertical field, as in *The Piano Lesson*, dynamically repeat the container and move in the direction of the surface, reiterating its flatness.

Extensions imply time and motion; it physically takes a period of time to move across an extended field. Japanese scrolls that are horizontal extensions are revealed in time and can be read in either direction. Extensions demonstrate an awareness of the world's multiple dimensions; as three-dimensional creatures, we have the ability to move side to side and up and down. Extensions can imply direction in a way that a regular rectangle can only hint at.

Any prolonged or exaggerated type of container presents its own set of fundamentals along with other basic design concepts. Maintaining compositional connections across an extended field is difficult. We are in danger of dividing the space into several regular rectangles or cutting off sections or compartmentalizing. And what happens to our rules about the dynamics of verticals and horizontals within rectangles?

9-1 Nicolas Poussin, *The Assumption of the Virgin*, oil on canvas

Courtesy of the National Gallery of Art, Washington, D.C.
(Gift of Mrs. Mellon Bruce)

A vertical extension is appropriate to this subject of the *Assumption of the Virgin*. The Assumption relates to a rise from earth to heaven. Our eyes move up the curves of the drapery on the tomb to the outside curving edges of the clouds, which brings us to the top. The vertical rise is reinforced by the vertical columns. Vertical extensions have been used in religious paintings for subjects such as the Deposition, The Last Judgment, The Crucifixion, and the Resurrection.

9-2 Henri Matisse, *The Blue Window*, 1911, autumn, oil on canvas
Courtesy of The Museum of Modern Art, New York
(Abby Aldrich Rockefeller Fund)

The blue field of color that fills the space is not a descriptive color, but acts as an element of continuity between the inside space and the space outside the window. The shape of each object joins in the flow from bottom to top. The table is not described in perspective; it is tilted to elongate the space.

9-3 Henri Matisse, *Piano Lesson*, 1916, oil on canvas

Courtesy of The Museum of Modern Art, New York
(Mrs. Simon Guggenheim Fund)

We enter the painting across the top of the piano and then
move vertically up the several architectural elements.
Matisse does not establish a ground plane for the background.
The female figure on the high chair floats above the
foreground and reinforces the vertical extension.

9-4 Pablo Picasso, *Nude Woman*, 1910, oil on canvas
Courtesy of the National Gallery of Art, Washington, D.C. (Ailsa Mellon Bruce Fund).
© S.P.A.D.E.M., Paris/V.A.G.A., New York, 1983
Picasso paints shifting and overlapping planes to move our eyes up the extended field. The contrast in light and dark establishes the meter and slight move back and forth into space.

9-5 H.L. Chu & Company Ltd., *Communicating with the Chinese Market*, folding brochure
H.L. Chu, art director, Hoi Ling Chu & Ben Perez, designers, New York
Mr. Chu designs a cover and four-panel folding brochure to open into a horizontal extention. The vertical panel of Chinese characters marks the first division; our eyes are then directed to the various objects and finally stop at another vertical column of Chinese characters. The objects are positioned to engage and activate the elongated horizontal container.

Communicating with the Chinese Market

与中国市场沟通

For centuries, the brush was one of the most important tools in China. With it, craftsmen created memorable designs and artifacts, merchants recorded their daily transactions, and scholars told of the intrigue of human events and the rise and fall of dynasties.

Learning to use the brush is not easy. First the student must be taught the basic techniques. Then he has to perfect his eye and hand through countless hours of practice. And finally, he must learn what to paint or write. For that, one almost has to be born a Chinese.

Because of the dedication, discipline and scholarship required, in feudal China, only an elite few ever learned to use this important tool of communication.

In this century, the brush has been largely replaced by modern implements and machinery. Still, if your company is among those exploring the trade opportunities in today's China, you should think about the time-honored brush as you prepare your promotional material. It is a symbol of the Chinese language and culture. And an understanding of the language and culture is the tool with which you can compel the attention of your trade partners.

9-6 April Greiman, *Art in Los Angeles*
April Greiman, art director and designer,
Los Angeles
There are three major compositional ideas that
move us up the page. First, the white triangle
of space in the bottom-left-hand corner
pushes us to read the second major element, the
wide (yellow) diagonal. Third, the horizontals
on the left edge of the page act like a
staircase, gradually moving us up the page.
Ms. Greiman truly understands the importance of
the edges of the container; they are all
taken into account.

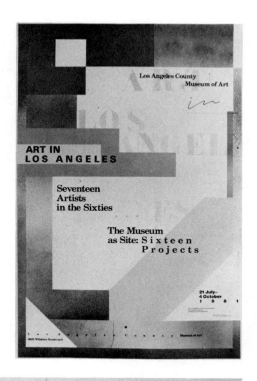

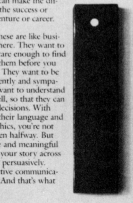

ith the young Chinese
ruggling with the
ring this new tool of
ion can make the dif-
een the success or
r venture or career.

Chinese are like busi-
ywhere. They want to
re, care enough to find
ut them before you
em. They want to be
lligently and sympa-
ey want to understand
well, so that they can
ed decisions. With
of their language and
graphics, you're not
n even halfway. But
age and meaningful
get your story across
and persuasively.
effective communica-
ut. And that's what
ut.

We at H.L.Chu & Company are
uniquely equipped to assist you
with your business ventures in
China. Our principal, Hoi Ling
Chu, is a native of China. He
received his design training both
in Hong Kong and in the United
States and holds degrees in both
Science and Art. Before establishing
his own practice, he was associated
with the internationally renowned
design consulting firm of
Chermayeff & Geismar Associates,
where he was responsible for a
wide range of award winning
projects for major corporations.

Aside from his thorough understanding of western design and
marketing concepts, he is steeped in
the culture he was brought up in.
He reads and writes Chinese. He
also speaks the official tongue as
well as two common dialects.

In addition, his personal skills are
complemented by those of some of
the most talented and authoritative
translators it is possible to assemble.

Working with us, you can be certain that your company literature
will be more than simply well designed. Words and images will be
carefully selected for their clear
meaning and for their unambiguous
appeal to the Chinese ear and eye.
We can help you avoid the awk-
wardness commonly associated with
this type of presentation. After all,
intelligent communication should
not be an insult to intelligence.

If you'd like to see some of our
work, please drop us a line with the
enclosed reply card or call collect at
(212) 751-3758. We'd like to show you
what we can do.

Hoi
Ling
Chu

朱凱陵

朱

9-7 Piet Mondrian, *Reclining Nude*, 1912
charcoal on paper
Courtesy of the Sidney Janis Gallery, New York
There are four major elongated curves that
describe the form; they also move us around the
container. They form a broken oval movement
within the horizontal extension. The shorter lines
set up a pace and describe the internal space.

9-8 Piet Mondrian, *Composition in Red, Yellow,
and Blue*, 1928,
oil on canvas
Courtesy of the Sidney Janis Gallery, New York
The scale of the forms in this painting, as well
as their placement, gives the illusion that the
painting is larger than it appears.

9-9 Robin Landa, *Objects of Desire*, 1978,
oil on canvas
(Private collection)
The fundamental compositional idea was that of a
cascade. Beginning with the drapery in the
lower-right we move up and around the objects,
following the implied curves. We read the
extended vision by looking down into the opening
of the teapot and up at the vase farthest back in
space.

the extended vertical

MATERIALS
* 11-by-15-inch white illustration board
* Rubber cement
* Black, light gray, medium gray, and dark gray Color-Aid paper

1. The aim is to move from the bottom to the top of the container.

2. On the vertically extended rectangle place the following variety of shapes and tones to create the greatest sense of rising from the bottom to the top:
* 1 light gray rectangular strip, 12 inches by 1 inch
* 1 black rectangular strip, 6 inches by 1 inch
* 1 dark gray rectangular strip, 4 inches by ¼ inch
* 1 dark gray rectangular strip, 3 inches by ½ inch
* 1 dark gray rectangular strip, 2 inches by ½ inch
* 1 medium gray rectangular strip, 3 inches by ¼ inch
* 1 medium gray rectangular strip, 2 inches by ¼ inch
* 1 middle gray 2-inch square
* 1 4-inch light gray circle
* 1 2-inch dark gray circle
* 4 black shapes of your choice, none of which is to exceed 2 inches in any dimension

Knowledge Gained

This project allows us to understand the interdependence of one element with another. The various shapes and tones must work together to move the viewer's eye from the bottom to the top. They must work together as players do on a team; each element is part of the greater composition.

How did you go about organizing the elements? Did you purposely position darker tones at the bottom and lighter tones at the top? Are all the shapes spread out evenly or are they clustered together? Did you find that if you moved one piece the dynamics of the entire design changed? Even if you placed the pieces without consciously questioning your actions, sit back

9-10 Student Work, *The Extended Vertical*
The ability to move the viewer's eye up and down an extended field is essential to advertising design and layout. The viewer must be able to read all the information that the advertiser wants to convey. It is the job of the designer to compose all the information and forms. Think of the various shapes and tones as pointers and directors to the top and to one another. They must communicate with one another, almost as if they were in conversation.

9-11 April Grieman, *Cal Arts View*,
promotional literature
April Greiman, art director & designer, Los Angeles
Photos, shapes, and type move our eyes up and around
the space. All the elements seem to float in space
and have a kinship of form to one another. For example,
the *V* in *View* is a simple triangle that reappears
as a decorative triangle at the top of the container.

and critique your design solution. Analyze the reasons for success.

In advertising design the vertical extension is often seen as a poster, folding brochure, announcement, or one-page advertisement. The horizontal extension is seen as a two-page spread in magazines or newspapers, brochures, folders, books, annual reports, and catalogs.

We have learned that extensions are appropriate for particular types of designs. Is a vertical extension more powerful than a horizontal extension? Are extensions more dynamic than regular rectangles or tondos? Dynamics and power are relative issues; they can be achieved in any container. But we do associate various containers with different roles and meanings just as we associate color with different meanings.

In advertising art, color has come to take on particular meanings—for example, the old cliché of pink for girls and blue for boys. Advertising artists understand that people make color associations. Phrases such as "the blues," "in the red," "he's yellow," or "green with envy" are under-

stood by everyone. Have you ever noticed that menthol cigarette packages are usually green or blue and white, or that the colors of products geared to a male audience are different from those geared to a female audience? These attitudes reflect certain elements inherent in the colors and their combinations.

The primary colors or *major triad* (red, blue, and yellow) is formed by inscribing an equilateral triangle within the color wheel. The characteristics of the triad are its brightness or intensity and its boldness. Red, blue, and yellow are all different and contrasting values in their pure states. This type of value relationship is a bold one, and it is not conducive to a small or intimate scale. The major triad has great visual carrying power; it is used for hard-sell merchandise. For example, it is often used for soap boxes, cereal boxes, and cheap magazines. The major triad is also associated with men's products and sports because of its visual boldness. In the past few years these hackneyed associations have become less rigid. We can infer from the ways in which the major triad has been used that the triad lends itself to powerful statements.

9-12 (left) Hans Arp, *Rectangles arranged according to the laws of chance,* 1916, collage
Courtesy of the Kunstmuseum, Kupferstichkabinett, Basle

Although Arp states in the title that forms were arranged according to the laws of chance, there seems to be a quite deliberate move from the bottom of the container to the top. The white space takes on rectangular shapes and the elongated white triangular shape at the right edge gives the rectangles an architectural feeling.

9-13 Kasimir Malewich, *Suprematist Painting,* oil on canvas
Stedelijk Museum, Amsterdam (Kasimir Malewich Suprematist painting collection)

The elements that seem to grow diagonally from the bottom left of the painting move us to the major diagonal axis in the center space. The overlapping of shapes increases the amount of tension.

125

9-14 (right) Alan Peckolick,
typographic designer, New York
Free Tues. Evenings
© Lubalin Peckolick Associates
The type is stacked to express the joint
availability of the three museums to the public
on Tuesday evenings. The *M*'s are wonderfully
designed as major forms that establish a repeat
and almost symmetrical order.

9-15 (below) Alan Peckolick,
typographic designer, New York
© 1900 Lubalin Peckolick Associates
Type can be designed to flow across an
extended field. The use of curves in the three
capital letters creates an elegant roll of
one letter into the next.

9-16 (bottom) General Exploration Co.
*The Second Annual GEX Family Picnic and
Reunion*, poster
Jack Summerford, art director, designer, &
artist, Summerford Design Firm, Inc.,
Dallas Texas
The three white shapes float across the
prolonged horizontal as if they were clouds
in the sky over the low horizon.

9-17 The Perfumer's Workshop Ltd.,
Rose Burst! Tea Rose
The diagonal movement of the copy is echoed by the burst of fragrance from the perfume bottle. We move up the well-placed rose petals, tassel, and bottle top. This vertical extension is extremely narrow in width, and yet by virtue of the placement and angle of the various shapes we feel the advertisement to be much wider than it actually is.

Rose
Burst!

Tea
Rose

The Perfumer's Workshop Ltd.
LONDON PARIS NEW YORK
© 1981 THE PERFUMER'S WORKSHOP, LTD.

the major triad &
the vertical extension

MATERIALS
- Color-Aid paper
- Gray or white illustration board
- Rubber cement
- Cutting tool

1. Spread out the Color-Aid pack and select the pure reds, blues, and yellows in all their value and chromatic variations. How can you tell if a hue is pure? Color is understood by comparison. Place the chosen hue among other similar hues. The one that appears to have little or no other hue in it is the pure one.

2. Since it is the nature of the major triad to be bold, because of its intrinsic brightness and contrasting values, we may choose to select the values and chromas of each component of the triad for these innate qualities. On the other hand, we may choose to select close values and low chromas and make the major triad soft and subtle. The type of values and chromas you select will play a major role in the color statement!

3. *The Design:* A vertical extension will be the container for this project. Design the color to read either up or down. The selection of values and chromas should govern the type of shapes, lines, and forms you use. For example, if you choose low chromas and light values you might want to use lines and shapes that are consonant. Think about the nature of the major triad and how it can best relate to a vertical extension. If the major triad is inherently bold, then perhaps your shapes should be large and bold. Perhaps angles will work well with this triad. Where do we see the major triad used most often? Cartoons, superhero comics, billboards, food packages, and sports magazines might be sources of design inspiration. Try to keep the design as abstract as possible; the

imagery should not overpower the color statement, but work with it.

Knowledge Gained
The major triad is a tool for understanding value and chroma relationships between colors. Its power is due to its inherent differences, and yet we have learned that these differences can be lessened by lightening the values and dropping the chromatic intensity. We have also been made to think about the psychological effects of hue, value, and chroma. The vertical extension has forced us to design color in a particular direction; color is a major compositional element. A nineteenth-century painter such as Delacroix constantly moves the viewer's eye around the painting by his color application.

The secondary colors or *minor triad* (orange, green, and violet) is often used for soft-sell merchandise; this color relationship reflects a subtler approach to advertising. The minor triad is often seen on such items as book jackets and cosmetic and perfume packages. These items are handled over a longer period of time than a news periodical or a can of soup. The battle for attention on a supermarket shelf would not be easily won by the minor triad. We tend to shop in a bookstore with a more reflective and thoughtful effort; therefore, subtlety can make itself felt. The minor triad has traditionally been associated with products for women: perfume boxes, women's magazines, cosmetic packages, and clothing. Only recently have designers become more courageous in their color choices. This is probably due to survey reactions from the general public to questions relating to color. Advertising agencies often are reluctant to take chances with a major color change without definite survey information.

the minor triad &
the horizontal extension

MATERIALS
- Color-Aid pack
- White or gray illustration board
- Rubber cement
- Cutting tool

1. Spread out the Color-Aid pack and select the pure oranges, greens, and violets in all their values and chromatic variations. **2.** The minor triad's inherent quality is softer than that of the major triad because it has a closer value range. The choice of particular values and chromas, whether they are contrasting or similar in value or intensity, will either make the minor triad bold or maintain its quiet nature. Make a conscious decision to do one or the other. **3.** *The Design:* In contrast to the shape of Project 9-3, we will execute this exercise in a horizontal extension. The three colors must interact and move the viewer's eye across the entire length of the extension. Billboards, two-page layouts in magazines and newspapers, scrolls, paintings, and brochures are all examples of horizontal extensions. How can color act to move the eye across an extended surface? Be careful not to create absolute subdivisions that disconnect vertically from one another.

Knowledge Gained
This project asks us to discriminate pure hues from compound hues and to identify them in their various value and chroma forms. Is there a difference in feeling between a low-chroma orange and a bright orange? How does a bright orange react against a low-chroma green or violet? Can an inherently quiet color harmony be made to scream? These are important questions; they must be answered through a process of trial and error in order to gain command over color in design. Color is not an isolated element. It is an integral design element. We should always look for or be aware of the use of the minor triad and other color theories in advertising art, fine art, and nature. Actively seeing color in all realms will widen our color vocabulary, and we will begin to understand the nature of color communication.

We begin our study of color with an exploration of various color definitions and theories stemming from the geometric color wheel. The geometric color wheel offers us simple color relationships which we can extend. We have just begun to understand the most often used harmonies: the major and minor triads. The members of each triad are taken from equidistant points on the color wheel, so that no two are adjacent or of the same family. The major triad is inherently bold, loud, and hard-edged and has great visual carrying power. But because we have learned to control value and chroma, we can make the major triad softer, more intimate, and soft-edged. If we keep its values light and close together and the chromas low, we can change its effect. The minor triad is inherently softer and more intimate, but it can be manipulated to change its effects as well.

If we take the major and minor triads and extend them individually to include their adjacent hues, we have a new color harmony. (See pp. 130–131.)

129

9-18 Robin Landa, *Pink Curves*, 1982, photograph
Courtesy of the Aaron Berman Gallery, New York
The curve of the drapery at the bottom of the container is set up to react to and answer the curve of the drapery holding the protruding object. The internal curves are held by these two major curves of the drapery; all the curves act together to compose the vertically extended space.

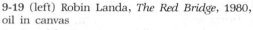

9-19 (left) Robin Landa, *The Red Bridge*, 1980, oil in canvas
Courtesy of the Aaron Berman Gallery, New York
Although this container is not an extremely prolonged horizontal extension, the horizontality is emphasized by the compositional element of a bridgelike curve upon which the vases rest. The downward curve of the drapery above the bridge pressures the forms in the middle of the composition. The two long vases on each edge lead to the two center vases and repeat the bridge.

9-20 Margaret Beaudette, S.C., *Fantastic Forest*, 1982, watercolor on paper
Collection of the artist, New York
Diagonals and curves move across this extended horizontal field and the contrasts in light and dark create depth.

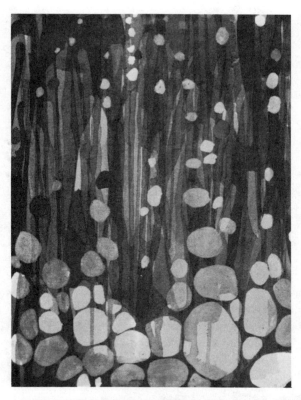

9-21 Margaret Beaudette, S.C., *Rolling Up*,
1980, watercolor on paper
Collection of the artist, New York
The title makes the design intention of this
work clear. The floating ovals direct
our eyes upward.

9-22 Brown-Forman Distillers Corporation,
Un Moment de Martell, magazine advertisement
© 1978, The Jos. Garneau Co., used by permission
The horizontal form of the piano creates a
dynamic response to the horizontal container.
The piano dynamically directs us to the
couple enjoying the cognac.

extended triads

MATERIALS
- Color-Aid pack
- Illustration board
- Rubber cement
- Cutting tool

1. Choose either the major triad or the minor triad.

2. Take each of the chosen triad's three component hues and find their analogous hues. The major triad is composed of R, Y, and B. The analogous colors to R are ROR and RVR. The analogous colors to Y are YGY and YOY. The analogous colors to B are BVB and BGB. Therefore, the extended major triad is ROR + R + RVR, YOY + Y + YGY, and BGB + B + BVB. The minor triad is comprised of O, G, and V. The analogous colors to O are OYO and ORO. The analogous colors to G are GYG and GBG. The analogous colors to V are VRV and VBV. Therefore, the extended minor triad is OYO + O + ORO, GYG + G + GBG, and VRV + V + VBV.

3. Do not spread the adjacent hues so far that they encompass the entire wheel. We are *not* combining the two triads; we are extending them to include their immediate analogous hues.

4. Maintain the overall feeling of the original triad. The extended triad must appear at first glance to have the look of either the major or minor triad. The extended triad's appearance should not be ambiguous.

5. *The Design:* The extension of the triads will prove to have a stabilizing effect. A square is a stable container. No side of a square is dominant in either a vertical or a horizontal direction. We could think of a square as the sum of a vertical extension and a horizontal extension. The design elements that come to mind when thinking of a square might be symmetry, order, parallelism, and focal points.

Knowledge Gained

We have expanded the coloristic range of the triads, thereby changing their inherent qualities. The addition of analogous hues to a triad begins to close the spatial gaps on the geometric color wheel, bringing the hues closer together. The major triad now has some minor properties simply by virtue of the fact that it has some orange, green, and violet in it. The minor triad now has some major properties because it has some red, yellow, and blue in it. We have learned to extend color relationships by imposing one theory on another. The theory of analogous harmony was imposed on the theory of the major and minor triads. We have also related the meaning of the new theory to an appropriate design concept.

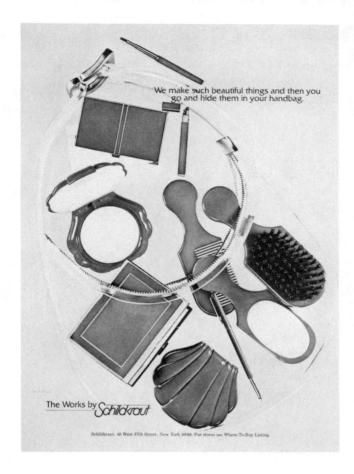

The Works by *Schildkraut*

9-23 Schildkraut, New York, *The Works by Schildkraut*, magazine advertisement
Altman, Stoller, Weiss Advertising Inc., New York
The products by Schildkraut illustrated in this ad are thoughtfully composed to move our eyes up and down the page, allowing us to read the written copy.

**ten
illusion &
atmosphere**

what is real?

The surface of a page is flat. The surface of a canvas is flat. If, on a flat surface, we draw or paint images that relate to things in the real world, we are creating an illusion. Three-dimensional solids cannot exist on a two-dimensional surface. But we can create an illusion of their existence. When we look at a painting by Goya or Corot, we forget the reality of the flat surface. How did these and many other artists throughout the history of art create such convincing illusions?

We can create the illusion of space behind the surface with the element of *value*. Gradations of light and dark values can create space. Very simply, dark values appear to be closer to us than lighter values. This visual illusion relates to the theory of atmospheric perspective popularized by Leonardo da Vinci in the sixteenth century. Leonardo observed that a spatial effect can be represented on a flat surface if one takes into account the effect the atmosphere has on color, form, and detail from a distance. The interposition of the atmosphere between the viewer and the objects seen causes forms to lose detail, blur at the edges, alter in hue, and diminish in intensity and value. The atmosphere has a graying effect on forms seen from a distance.

10-1 Piet Mondrian, *Composition*, 1921, oil on canvas
Courtesy of the Sidney Janis Gallery, New York
Mondrian asserts the inherent flat reality of the canvas.

136

10-2 Attributed to Francisco Goya, *The Bullfight*, oil on canvas

The painterly quality of this work contributes to the creation of atmosphere and distance.

10-3 Jean-Baptiste-Camille Corot, *The Eel Gatherers*, oil on canvas

Corot's range of grays is extremely subtle; it is because of this narrow range that we so greatly believe the illusion. The narrow range of grays creates an air-filled space with light values acting as reflections of sunlight.

10-4 Joseph Mallord William Turner, *The Slave Ship*, oil on canvas

Although the subject of this painting is a historical event that occurred in 1783, the artist stresses the atmospheric effects to the point where the atmosphere almost obliterates the reading of the subject matter. The turbulent atmosphere is appropriate to the scene.

10-5 Robin Landa, *The Ribbon*, 1982, photograph
Courtesy of the Aaron Berman Gallery, New York
Photography, as a medium, is highly dependent upon the manipulation of light and shadow for the creation of an illusion. All of the photographer's tools—camera, lenses, film, lights, and subject matter—can aid in the creation of light and dark relationships.

planes of value

MATERIALS
- Black and white tempera paint
- Brushes
- White index cards
- 10-inch-square white illustration board

1. Paint 10 different grays in a range from black to white on 1-inch squares.
2. Place them on the square board to create the maximum amount of space and depth from their relationships.

Knowledge Gained

The ability to make judgments about where a particular value is in space in relation to another value is crucial to illusionism.

10-6 Student Work, *Planes of Value*
The ability to judge where a particular value is in space in relation to another value is crucial to illusionism.

atmospheric perspective

MATERIALS
- Black and white tempera paint
- 10-inch-square white illustration board
- Brush
- Pencil
- Ruler

1. Divide the board into four equal boxes. Then divide it once again by drawing two lines through the center and from corner to corner.

2. Paint on the divided planes a graded series of values that make the planes recede or advance.

3. The values can be darker at the outside edges or in the center. The variation is up to you.

Knowledge Gained

This project differs from Project 10-1 in that the spatial effect is helped along by gradations. The blending of one value into another increases the amount of atmosphere. If you choose to have all the values darken at the center, the space will look different than it will if all the values are dark at the edges. The space tends to flatten if the position of the darker values are alternated between the outside edges and the center.

In previous chapters, we have dealt with spatial dynamics related to the action of linear movement and shape interplay. But generally we relate our vision of space to a change in values as we encounter space in daily life. Black and white television, video, film, and the photographic reproductions found in newspapers, books, magazines, and the photodocumentation that accompanies us from our first baby shots and family pictures all depend upon value for their illusionism. If you have ever seen a black and white photo emerge in the developer, you will have observed that it begins with equal values emerging on every plane that is not pure light. Then gradually, there is a shift as the various values that create the illusion of volumes in space emerge.

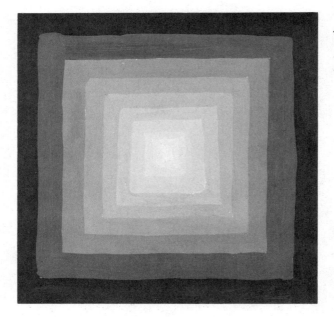

10-7 Student Work,
Atomspheric Perspective
Does the center appear to recede or advance when the dark values are at the outside edges?

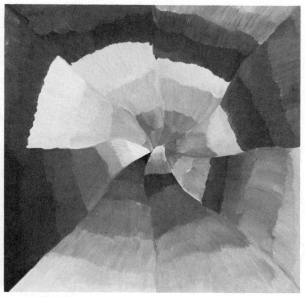

10-8 Student Work, *Atmospheric Perspective*
The space flattens when the dark and light graded planes are alternated. This especially occurs when the edge of each plane is clearly defined.

10-9 Student Work, *Atmospheric Perspective*
Although there is a variation of the graded planes, atmosphere is achieved because of the painterly application of the values and the deliberately curved edges of the planes. Curving the edges of the planes creates volume.

141

field density

MATERIALS
- 8-inch-square white paper
- Variety of pencils

1. *Hatching* is a technique that is used to create value or atmosphere by applying closely spaced parallel lines. When another group of lines crosses the first at an angle, it is called *crosshatching*.

2. Build up a dense field of value with hatching and crosshatching.

3. The hatching may be in any direction. You may use a ruler or draw freehand.

4. Vary the density of the field at different areas of the container. Some areas should be more open and some should be more dense.

5. The lines should eventually create the illusion of atmosphere.

Knowledge Gained

When one group of lines crosses another one, it pushes the first group back into space. If groups of lines constantly cross one another, the space behind the surface will seem to constantly move farther back. An illusion of deep atmospheric space is created. The flat surface is transformed into a dense field through the constant buildup of closely spaced lines. Varying the density of hatched lines in different areas of the container gives the viewer a sense of shifting air and a feeling that the veil of atmosphere is penetrable.

COLOR AND ILLUSIONISM

The geometric color wheel offers us simple color relationships which we can extend and push and pull into various harmonies. We understand that color is relative, depending upon its surroundings and design for its appearance. We have learned to read hue, value, and chroma. Can we now use color to create the illusion of space?

We know that variations and gradations of value create spatial illusions. Value is one of the three qualities of color. Let us now add hue and chroma and create space. But instead of using a color theory from the geometric color wheel, we will explore another set of color relationships.

In chapter seven we learned to see colors as points of focus. Bright hues become special when surrounded by low-chroma hues. But where are these hues in space? Are the bright hues in front of the low-chroma hues? Do warm colors move in front of cool colors?

Pages 143–45:

10-10, 10-11, *Versations*, book
Warren Lehrer, author, art director, designer, & typographer, Jan Baker and Wentao Cheng, letterers, Lehrer/Baker, publisher, Stanford, Connecticut
The buildup of letters over one another creates a density of atmosphere on the surface. Usually letters on a page reassert the inherent flatness of the page, but in these works the letters create space and depth by virtue of their placement and the layering of the letters.

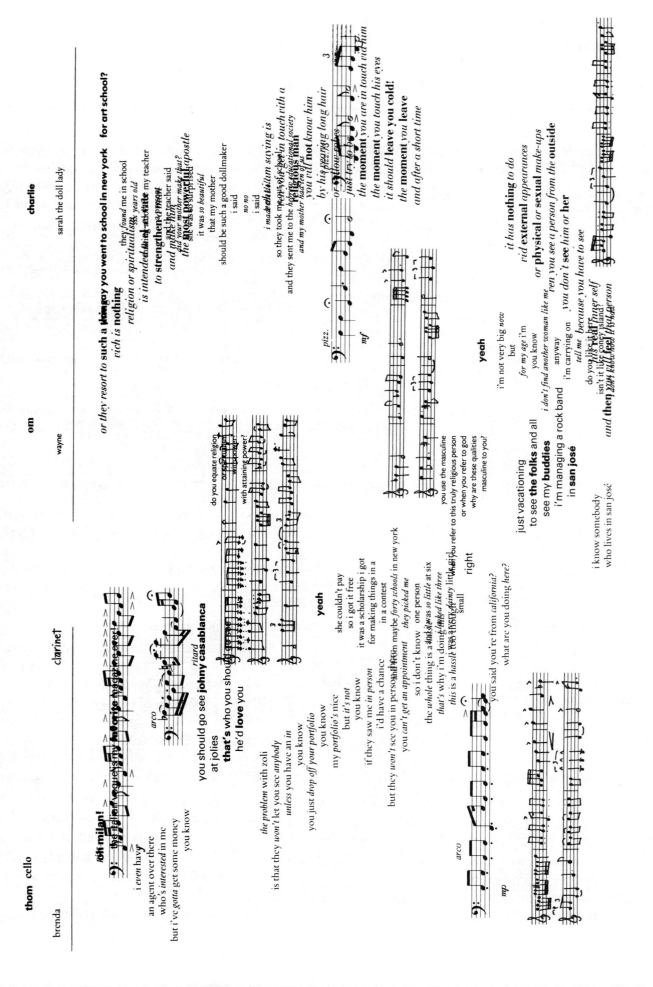

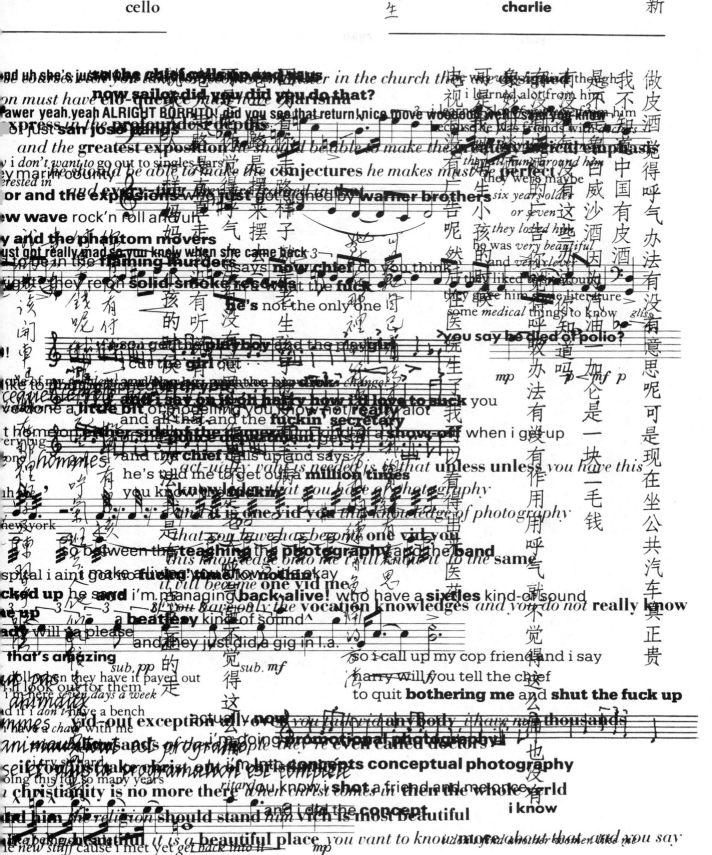

10-12 Alberto Giacometti, *Paysage*, 1960,
oil on canvas

Courtesy of the Sidney Janis Gallery, New York

Although Giacometti's lines do not lose their
character as lines, the constant searching out of
forms in space with lines creates atmosphere.

the push & pull
of color in space

MATERIALS
- Acrylic or casein paint in the following colors: burnt umber, ultramarine blue, alizarin crimson, Naples yellow, white, cadmium red, cadmium yellow, thalo green
- 11-by-15-inch white illustration board
- Brush and palette

Note: A tempera set of red, yellow, blue, black, and white may be substituted if the student does not wish to purchase this additional palette of colors.

1. Paint three bright hues, such as cadmium red, thalo green, and cadmium yellow, at different points on the vertically held container. The position of the three bright hues should activate the space of the container.

2. By placing different grays mixed from the remaining hues around these three bright hues, push and pull the bright hues into different positions in space.

3. For example, the cadmium red area may seem to come forward in front of the thalo green and cadmium yellow. Various gray mixtures may have the ability to push the red back in space.

4. Get as many grays out of this palette as possible. Feel free to do visual experimentation. This is an extremely open-ended project.

5. The placement of the bright hues in the container will affect our reading of their position in space.

Knowledge Gained

The determination of where a particular color sits in space is perhaps the most difficult job of a colorist. Whether we are aware of it or not, we are always placing colors in space. If we can learn to control the position of a color in space, we can create the illusion of space. It is really not a matter of whether an individual hue is bright or dull, warm or cool; rather it is a matter of the relationships among the hues with various characteristics. How does a cool hue affect a warm hue in terms of their position in space? Can a very opaque, dull hue be located in front of a bright hue? What is the relationship between transparent colors and opaque colors in terms of space? These questions must be answered by experimenting with different palettes and color relationships. The final decision about the relationships of colors and how they can create space, illusion, or atmosphere is always in the visual work, not in the conceptual theory.

close values

MATERIALS
- Tempera or acrylic paint
- Brush
- Palette
- 10-inch-square white illustration board

1. Divide the board into 10 boxes.

2. In each box, paint a different hue that is near to white in value.

3. All the hues should be extremely light and equal in value, but different in hue.

4. From a distance the board should appear white. Up close we should be able to distinguish ten different hues.

Knowledge Gained

Atmosphere can be created by keeping hues close in value. Artists such as Matisse and Bonnard utilized this theory. This project fosters the ability to discriminate minute shifts in hue.

The creation of illusion on a two-dimensional surface is an abstract concept. It is abstract because three-dimensional forms cannot exist on a two-dimensional surface. The surface is flat. That is a real concept. In Project 4-2 we tied up the surface of the page, and in Project 10-3 we opened up the surface with a veil of atmosphere. If we compare these Projects we can see the dynamic range that the two-dimensional surface can offer.

In earlier chapters we learned that we could create space with line and linear volumes. If we can create volume and space with line, can we heighten the illusion by adding value? Will the reality of the flat surface be denied more forcefully with planes of value than it was with the linear definitions of volumes?

Plate 1
Robin Landa, *Sugar and Spice*, 1982, photograph
Courtesy of the Aaron Berman Gallery, New York
The forms in this photograph are symbolic and
are therefore kept in sharp focus. We can
examine each object because of the clarity of
focus, but it is the composition that
directs our eyes and sets up the mood and
environment. The center wedding ornament,
a circular force, is an element of connection
that organizes the space.

Plate 2
Robin Landa, *Objects of Desire: The Horse*,
1978, oil on canvas
Courtesy of the Aaron Berman Gallery
Since the nineteenth century, artists have been
interested in the exploration of
perceptual space. How can we communicate the
full vertical length of our visions to
others? How can we tell the viewer that we
looked up, center, and down?

Plate 3
Giotto, *The Betrayal of Christ*,
fourteenth century, fresco
Courtesy of the Arena Chapel, Padua, Italy
The dynamic diagonals of the staves and sticks
lead to the kiss of betrayal. Our eye is
directed to the formal center of the painting,
as well as to the dramatic focal point.

Shiseido, *Practice Shiseido*
Shiseido, *Practice Shiseido*
(magazine advertisement)
The figure moves with the flow of the tondo, and
the two circular forms within create repetitions of
the outer circle. The flowing design is
appropriate for the product.

Plate 5
Christian Dior Perfumes, Inc., *Dioressence*
Texture can be implied by the use of patterns.
A rich variety of designed textures can
have a graphic impact.

Plate 6 (left)
Student Work, Project 8-7, *Analogous Harmony*
Volume is created by the overlapping of circular
forms and curves. The hue variation is
subtle and the value range is close, which helps
to enhance the harmonious feeling.

Plate 7 (facing page)
PepsiCo Diet Pepsi, *Cruise/Anthony*
(advertising campaign)
Reprinted with permission of ©PepsiCo, Inc., 1981
All visuals in this print and television campaign
make use of cropped images. It uses closeup
shots, and even though all figures and
objects are cut off or cropped in some way, we

SINGERS: Now you see it

Now you don't.

Here you have it

Here you won't.

Diet Pepsi one small calorie, ahh!

Now you see it

Now you don't.

That great Pepsi taste

Diet Pepsi

won't go to your waist.

Now you see it

Now you don't.

Diet Pepsi one small calorie, ahh!

Now you see it

Now you don't.

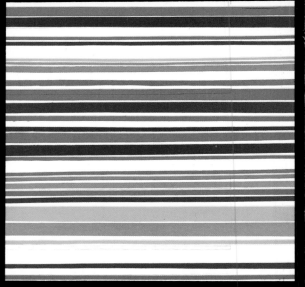

Plate 8 (left)
April Greiman, art director & designer,
Los Angeles
Firm: April Greiman, Los Angeles, California
The use of cast shadows behind forms pushes
the forms forward in space and increases the
illusion of three dimensions
on a two-dimensional surface.

Plate 9 (above)
Student Work, Project 2-4, *Chromatic Recession*
and Advancement: A Warp
Complements can enhance or nullify one another
Their interaction can create spatial shifts
and swells.

Plate 10 (below)
Student Work, Project 9-5, *Extended Triads*
This extended major triad retains the inherent
bold qualities of the major combination.

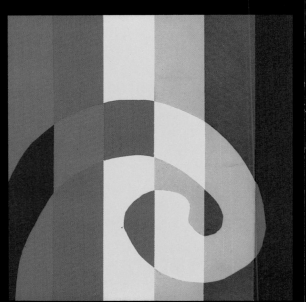

volume through value

MATERIALS
- Black spray paint
- White paper
- Illustration board

1. Redo Project 5-2 in terms of planes of value instead of linear volumes.
2. With black spray paint and large sheets of white paper, gradually spray about five sheets from near white to near black with the mist of the spray can.
3. Then enlarge your original project design and turn each plane with a particular value so that the illusion of three-dimensional volumes is heightened.
4. If you wish the space to be logical, make sure that the light source is constant. For example, the right side of volumes will be light in value. If you desire ambiguous spatial relationships, the light source should be inconsistent.

Knowledge Gained
We know that each type of container has its own character and identity. But what about internal space? Can we have different types of illusion? Line, linear volumes, color, and value can create internal space and deny the concrete reality of the surface. Each type of illusion has its own characteristics and potential for communication, and should be viewed in relation to the artist's intention, time period, subject matter, and philosophy.

10-13 Student Work, *Volume Through Value*
Planes of value give great volume to forms in space. Light and shadow are natural to the way we see and work in the medium of design and painting to represent reality on a two-dimensional surface.

10-14 Automatic Data Processing, Inc.,
Clifton, New Jersey, *Focusing on Your Benefits*,
promotional literature
Rachel Katzen, art director & designer
The illusion of space is created by the
overlapping of numbers and by shifts from thin
forms to thick forms.

10-15 Kurt Schwitters, *Lichtkegel Merz 2009*,
1925, pencil
Courtesy of the Sidney Janis Gallery, New York
Shifts in space and an illusion of depth are
created by the technique of small splotches
of black, applied in varying concentrations.

10-16 (facing page, top)
Champion International Corporation,
Champions of the Future, 1981,
appointment calendar
Bruce Blackburn, design director, Danne &
Blackburn, Inc., New York
The shift from light to dark or dark to light
creates atmosphere as well as symbolizing a
movement towards the future.

10-17 (facing page, bottom)
The Hennegan Company, Wheaton, Illinois,
Photography Manarchy/Lithography Hennegan,
poster
Jeff Barnes, designer, Jeff Barnes Design
The pattern of light and shadow on forms can
break into the appearance of abstraction
and simultaneously retain identity as
the illumination of recognizable forms.

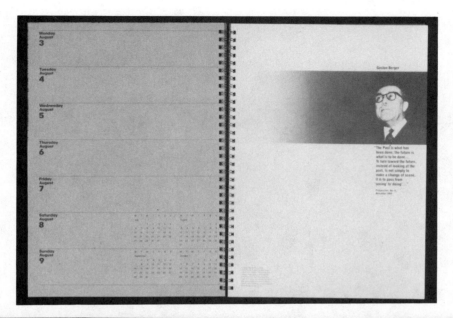

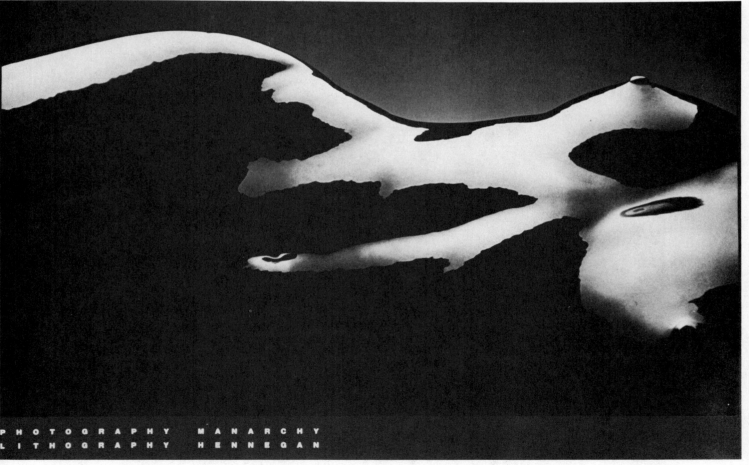

10-18 Georges de la Tour, *The Repentant Magdalen*, 1640, oil in canvas

Courtesy of the National Gallery of Art, Washington, D.C. (Ailsa Mellon Bruce Fund)

The candle behind the skull is the only source of light and illuminates the forms in the painting. The light source creates dramatic contrasting relationships of light and dark.

10-19 Princess Marcella Borghese, Inc.,
Di Borghese. The Perfume of the Night,
magazine advertisement
The light in this ad appears to originate
from the bottle of perfume, which illuminates
the figure.

153

10-20 Drexel Burnham Lambert, *Investor Services*, corporate literature
Keri Keating, designer, Colin Forbes & Dan Friedman, art directors,
Pentagram Design, New York
Graded plans of light and dark that overlap one another create
space behind the surface. This technique is unusual in
corporate literature and is highly effective.

Commodities

Hedging facilities, professional commodity management services and timely research have established for Drexel Burnham Lambert a substantial and widely recognized position as a multinational futures broker to the world commodity trade.

Research

Drexel Burnham Lambert's commodity futures trading expertise is supported by research and information capabilities, including technical and fundamental analysis reports, plus up-to-the-minute market intelligence available through a sophisticated communications system.

Commercial Hedging Services

Professional commercial hedging services represent the major part of Drexel Burnham Lambert's efforts to help commercial clients lessen their exposure to price risk. In major offices throughout the world special full-service commodity trade groups provide hedging facilities.

Grains
A team of specialists in Chicago, led by one of the most respected names in the grain futures business, provides hedging expertise for agricultural producers, merchants and processors worldwide. Clients range from soybean growers in Brazil to corn importers in Europe to wheat millers in America.

Metals
As the only U.S. brokerage firm with comprehensive trading operations in the metals centers of New York and London, Drexel Burnham Lambert serves producers, fabricators and dealers around the world. Our unique dual market capability allows us to maintain a dominant position as a commodity broker to the international metal trade.

Coffee, Sugar and Cocoa
Expert trade units provide coordinated services to major processors, producers and dealers from strong bases in New York and London.

Financial Futures
A combination of Drexel Burnham Lambert's financial futures, corporate bond and government securities expertise enables us to provide corporations and financial institutions with hedging facilities in the futures markets in financial instruments. In particular, we are active in treasury bills, treasury bonds and GNMA futures.

Foreign Exchange
To assist our worldwide clients hedge their currency exposure, a core team of foreign exchange traders in New York maintains a trading presence in both the futures markets and the interbank market. Trading facilities in London and Hong Kong give us access to the interbank market around-the-clock, as well as around the globe.

Other Markets
Drexel Burnham Lambert can also serve the needs of hedging clients in the meat, cotton, lumber and other commodity futures markets.

Investor Services

In response to the increasing appeal of futures trading as a means to offset inflation, Drexel Burnham Lambert has significantly increased its commitment to providing professional commodity execution, research and management services to individual and institutional investors.

DBL Futures Advisory Corp.
This subsidiary provides commodity asset management services to individuals and institutions.

Commodity Asset Management Program
Developed to offer substantial individual and institutional investors the opportunity to participate in the potential rewards of commodity futures trading through a computer-assisted trading system. This program was designed and is continually monitored by a professional and highly experienced team of money managers well acquainted with the commodity futures markets.

Investment Management

In response to increasing investment complexity, Drexel Burnham Lambert has instituted a number of specialized investment management programs, designed to provide investors with the benefits of professional expertise coupled with on-the-scene supervision.

Drexel Burnham Lambert Investment Advisors

Drexel Burnham Lambert Investment Advisors manage over $1 billion of assets for clients, who include wealthy individuals and families, as well as institutional accounts, such as employee benefit funds, endowment funds, insurance companies and mutual funds. Accounts are managed on either a discretionary or advisory basis for equity, fixed income or balanced portfolios.

Balanced Portfolio Management
Makes use of the full economic and research capabilities of the firm in the decision-making process.

Fixed Income Asset Management
Serves portfolios which consist exclusively of bonds and preferred stocks.

Worldwide Investment Management
Offers investors the opportunity to diversify assets internationally.

Quantitative Portfolio Management
Allows equity investors to benefit from the application of Modern Portfolio Theory to investment decisions.

Personal Asset Control Evaluation

PACE is a complete financial planning service designed to facilitate estate and income tax planning, budget planning, retirement planning, education planning, and emergency planning for the individual.

Corporate and Executive Services

This department provides special investment services to substantial individuals, corporations and corporate executives. In addition, the group is equipped to assist holders of restricted securities in the effective sale of their shares.

Fund Management

International Funds
Allow non-U.S. investors to participate in internationally diversified growth funds.

Worldwide Special Fund N.V. Worldwide Securities Limited
International growth funds with globally diversified portfolios specifically designed for non-U.S. investors.

Winchester Overseas Ltd.
A commodity futures trading fund for non-U.S. investors.

The Drexel Burnham Fund
An open-end no-load mutual fund seeking growth and income.

Drexel Bond Debenture Trading Fund
An income-oriented, closed-end fund consisting primarily of a diversified portfolio of fixed-income securities.

Managed Options Program

Our Managed Options Program is designed to assist individual and institutional investors to improve portfolio performance with reduced risk through the utilization of suitable option strategies.

**eleven
collage & texture**

how do we make these elements work?

At the beginning of this century new ideas about reality emerged. The dominant one that influenced artists was the idea that time never stopped—that life was always in motion. The still photograph did not truly reflect reality as we experienced it. Neither did the art of the past. So the artists attempted to create works that would more truly reflect life and its constant movement.

One primary mode of expression was the shifting of planes on the two-dimensional surface. This creates an illusion of movement on the flat surface without becoming involved with the rendering of solid closed unbroken form. It was as if time and motion were shattering solids to make them move in space. As this artistic movement, called *Cubism*, developed, the painting mode expanded. The representational and atmospheric qualities of traditional art evaporated and the shifting of planes filled the container, forcing a greater sense of surface. Overlaps of forms became shifts of one surface over another and artists actually began to paste bits of newspaper and other materials such as playing cards, oilcloth, and rope on the surface of paintings. The fact that an artist can paste materials on the surface of a painting testifies to the inherent flatness of the surface. The act of cutting and pasting materials to the two-dimensional surface, which we call *collage*, merges actual reality with the illusion of the painted surface.

Picasso was one of the artists most involved with the redefinition of painting. In 1912 he executed a work entitled *Still Life with Chair Caning* that incorporated collage into painting. He pasted a piece of oilcloth to the canvas surface instead of rendering the texture through illusion. This was the beginning of a mode of expression which has taken hold of the imagination of artists continually up to the present day. Collage presented an open-ended set of possibilities in art that had never before been explored.

The formal means of shifting planes on the surface, collage and the manipulation of elements on the flat surface, broke with

11-1 Georges Braque, *Homage to J. S. Bach*, 1912, oil on canvas
Courtesy of the Sidney Janis Gallery, New York
Cubism challenged traditional painting and brought into question
fundamental ideas about reality and art that artists still contemplate.
Cubism broke with traditional attitudes about the development
of space on the two-dimensional surface. Although artists in the
nineteenth century, such as Monet and Manet, had been exploring
perceptual space and questioning the depiction of reality, Cubism
was more radical in its departure from the accepted role of art.

traditional art and involved new philosophies about life and art. This mode essentially states that the two-dimensional surface is flat, a concrete reality, and that there is no need for the illusionism that formed the basis of Western painting for centuries. With this idea the picture plane becomes almost sacred. To puncture an illusionistic hole in the plane is a vindictive criticism of this philosophy. Painting became a new metaphor for reality. Art no longer had to obey the laws of tradition. Photography could record the world of real things and freed painting to explore new realms. Painting turned toward introspection.

Art could be about art. It could raise philosophical questions without the use of representation and narrative art. It could express ideas about time, motion, truth, and reality through formal means rather than literal symbols or stories. The formal elements of art were now the subject of art. Collage, letter forms, and the use of shifting planes are all formal elements of the Cubist vocabulary that set up an enormous range of design dynamics for the fine artist and the commercial artist. We have the freedom to merge the two-dimensional surface with three-dimensional materials, thicknesses, and textures. This allows us to vary the texture of the surface of a design or painting and to create illusions of volume without having to illustrate or render that volume. It also brings us back to the surface and reiterates the flatness of the picture plane.

159

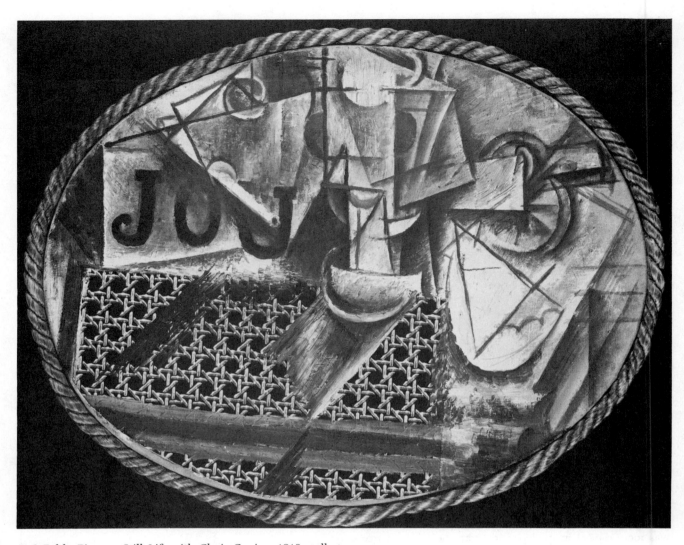

11-2 Pablo Picasso, *Still Life with Chair Caning*, 1912, collage
Courtesy of the Picasso Museum, Paris. © S.P.A.D.E.M., Paris/V.A.G.A.,
New York, 1983

Picasso pasted a piece of patterned oilcloth to the surface of this
canvas in 1912. The pattern, adhered to the surface,
eliminated the need for him to render the chair caning pattern.
This action began a technique and ultimately a philosophy about the
role of illusionism and about the inherent flat nature of
the two-dimensional surface that would engage the interest of the
entire art world. Pasting materials to the two-dimensional surface
maintains the flat surface of the canvas.

11-3 Kurt Schwitters, *Merz 13A Oval*, 1919,
oil on collage
Courtesy of the Sidney Janis Gallery, New York
Artists picked up on the Cubist and collage
impulse and pasted many different materials to
the surface of the canvas. Some materials
were three-dimensional, such as coins or buttons.

160

161

letter collage

MATERIALS
- 10-inch-square illustration board
- Rubber cement
- Cutting tool
- Newspapers
- Magazines

1. Create a design by cutting and shifting letters.

2. Overlapping may be used to create the feeling of spatial movement.

3. Think about the scale of the letter forms: large shapes vs. small shapes.

4. Black and white paint may be used in addition to the cut paper.

5. Letters should move and create spatial shifts. Letters should not form readable words.

6. Think about utilizing figure/ground principles as well as value. Value might include the thickness or blackness of an area, the grays created by the black and white print, and how the grays create areas that seem close to or far away from the surface.

Knowledge Gained

The type of space the collage creates is similar to true figure/ground design in that it is constantly bringing us back to the surface. Even though there are shifting planes or overlapping forms, the move into space is slight. The finished design relates to our tactile sense because textures and materials are pasted on the surface. Learning to move elements and place them on the surface is a compositional approach. Placing elements on a page is as important compositionally as making direct marks with paint or pencil on the surface.

11-4 Student work, *Letter Collage*

11-5 Kurt Schwitters, *A Nice Button*,
1947, collage
Courtesy of the Sidney Janis Gallery, New York
Texture brings our eye to the surface and
keeps it there. Textures were always
illusionistically rendered in traditional
painting. Collage allowed artists to
dispense with rendering, enabling them to
paste materials directly to the surface.

texture: indirect marks

11-6 Jean Dubuffet, *Femme au Sexe Oblique*, 1950, oil on panel
Courtesy of the Sidney Janis Gallery, New York
Dubuffet scratches into the impasto surface of thick paint, creating a texture on texture.

MATERIALS
- Tracing paper
- Soft pencils
- Crayons
- 10-inch-square white illustration board
- Rubber cement
- Cutting tool
- Black paint or India ink

1. Using tracing paper and pencils or crayons, take rubbings from textured surfaces. For example, place a comb under tracing paper and pick up the texture with the side of a crayon, or place tracing paper on a tree trunk or rock and take a rubbing.
2. Create several blottings by dipping interesting objects into black paint or India ink and blot them repeatedly on tracing paper.
3. Divide the 10-inch-square illustration board into nine boxes and choose a variety of rubbings and blottings to fit into the ruled boxes.
4. Think about the edges between the different textures and how they relate to one another.

Knowledge Gained
Rubbings and blottings are indirect marks. The use of textures expands the range of visual excitement and includes our sense of touch. Texture can act as a purely formal element or as a sign for a representational object. Texture and collage can set up spatial ambiguity and surface tension; they also have the potential to be witty.

The building of volumes out of chiseled or shifted planes was relatively tonal in the work of Picasso and Braque. They shifted tones or values from warm to cool by relying on a palette of white, black, yellow ochre, and other earth tones. Other followers of the Cubist philosophy transposed the idiom into color. They were the *Orphists*. Planes of color, bright and varied in hue, could shift against one another, creating spiraling disks or forms in space.

color collage

MATERIALS
- Color-Aid pack
- Gray illustration board
- Magazines
- Found paper
- Rubber cement
- Cutting tool

1. Using Color-Aid paper and found colored paper or materials create a collage whose design and focus is on a specific color statement. The color statement may reflect theories that we have studied, such as analogous harmony or the major triad, or you may wish to explore color on a completely experimental level.

2. Remember to combine design principles with color relatedness. The design should be thought of in relation to the color theory and should enhance the color statement.

3. Hue, value, and chroma should work hand in hand with texture, scale, composition, and the creation of space. They will have effects on one another.

Knowledge Gained
Design and color often rely on one another for a successful final solution. Cubism and collage are probably the major impulses behind twentieth-century art. These modes have opened up brand-new avenues of thought and possibilities that artists are still exploring and discovering. The questioning of reality and of the ways which we can translate it into painting and design is certainly intriguing.

**twelve
communication
through
design**

how can we get a message across?

12-1 Student Work, *Fat*
The design and typeface should
be appropriate to the meaning
of a word or phrase.

168

We have learned to communicate. Our parents put a bottle in front of us, and we reached for it. We communicated. We made funny noises and our parents delighted in extracting "mama" and "dada" out of them. As we grew, we learned more and more vocabulary, perhaps even inventing our own with family and friends. We learned that certain gestures of the body were friendly and others unfriendly.

All of this is communication. As children we utilize body language, voice, language, and intuitive psychology. These elements add up to a complex network of references and meanings that make up a system of communication. Some of us use communication systems better than others, but we all use them.

Just as there is an elaborate structure for language and physical communication, there is an elaborate structure for visual communication. We can communicate through design. It is essential for us, as designers, to think visually. Designers have to be able to inform, persuade, motivate, and direct their audiences. This means that the designer must have a wealth of information about visual communication at his or her fingertips, including some sense of psychology and a good knowledge of the written language.

A designer must be intelligent, knowledgeable, quick thinking, industrious, up-to-date on the latest trends and technology, and *well versed in the design medium*. We must always be aware of the world around us, the environment, people's needs, publications, architecture, packaging, commercials, and new ideas. Inspiration can come from anything and anywhere.

Design is a system that orders and translates reality and ideas into meaningful units which are intelligible and communicative. There must be an underlying structure in a design message that communicates to us on deeper levels than the literal message. In order to convey literal messages, the designer must think abstractly, in terms of design elements. For example, if we wanted to communicate the word *fat*, we might think of designing it in a tondo utilizing thick, round, curved letters.

The following series of exercises will demonstrate ways to utilize design elements in visual communication.

figure ground & communication

MATERIALS
- Black and white tempera paint
- Illustration board
- Brush
- Paint

PART I

1. Design a word purely for the purpose of figure/ground space. The aim is to design not only the letters but the space in between them.

2. You may use conventional typefaces or invent your own.

3. The word does not have to make literal sense. For example, you may choose certain letters for their particular shapes, rather than choosing them for their literal meaning. The word may be in any language.

PART II

1. Design your name so that it is readable but still utilizes figure/ground relationships.

2. Design the space in between the letters as well as the letters themselves.

Knowledge Gained

Becoming conscious of the negative space makes us design the total container as one organic field, rather than as separate shapes. Shapes become more dynamic when the entire space is considered. A message can only have power when the entire container is thought of as important.

12-2 Student Work, Figure/Ground & Communication, *Gas*
The design of type can be unusual in its placement and still be readable.

12-3 Alan Peckolick, typographical designer, New York, *Phoenix House*, logo
© Lubalin Peckolick Associates
The spaces between the letters are as important as the letter forms themselves. This method of designing gives power to the positive forms of the letters.

12-4 Student Work
Figure/Ground & Communication,
Renee

12-5 Student Work, Figure/Ground &
Communication, *Mary*

word communication

MATERIALS
- Tempera paints
- Markers
- Collage materials

1. Communicate the meaning of a word both literally and formally within the design medium, using figure/ground principles.

2. Formal elements such as placement within the container, texture, figure/ground space, line, color, volume, focal point, and balance can aid the literal meaning of the word. Composition is very important to the power of communication.

3. Be sure that the formal elements are appropriate to the meaning of the word. For example, the word *low* might be communicated very simply by placing it at the bottom of the page and using short letters.

4. You may use any materials that are appropriate to the meaning of the word.

Knowledge Gained

In order to communicate the meaning of a word, we must define the word in design terms. Words obviously have literal meanings, but we can give them formal definitions as well. Space can be designed to communicate meaning. For example, if we have a group of elements crowded together on one side of a container and a single element on the other side, we might read the composition as communicating isolation.

12-6 Alan Peckolick, typographic designer, New York, *Rush Dance Company*
© Lubalin Peckolick Associates
We feel the sensation of graceful, creative movement in the design of the word *Rush*, appropriate for a dance company.

12-7 Alan Peckolick, typographic designer, New York, *Beards*
© Lubalin Peckolick Associates

MARRIAGE

12-8 Herb Lubalin, typographic designer
Marriage, 1975, logo
© Lubalin Peckolick Associates
The linking of the R's in *Marriage*
symbolizes the union the people
in such a relationship.

12-9 Alan Peckolick,
typographic designer, New York
Toes Clothes
© *Lubalin Peckolick Associates*

12-10 Herb Lubalin, typographic designer
Grumbacher, 1979, logo
© Lubalin Peckolick Associates
The logo for Grumbacher, an art supply company,
is appropriately rendered with letter forms
that look like paint squeezed out of a tube.

Families

A READER'S DIGEST
PUBLICATION

12-11 Herb Lubalin, typographic designer
Families, 1980, logo
© Lubalin Peckolick Associates
Shortening the length of the second "li" in
familes implies three different heights that
might be found in a family of three. Dotting the
"l" in families does not interfere with our
reading of the word.

BEST

12-12 Best Products, Co., *Best*,™ logo
Thomas H. Geismar, art director &
designer, Chermayeff & Geismar Associates
New York

173

12-13 Student Work, Word Communication: *Low*

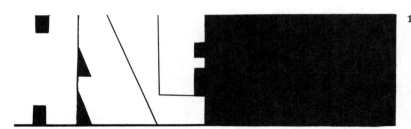

12-14 Student Work, Word Communication: *Half*

12-15 Student Work, Word Communication: *Split*

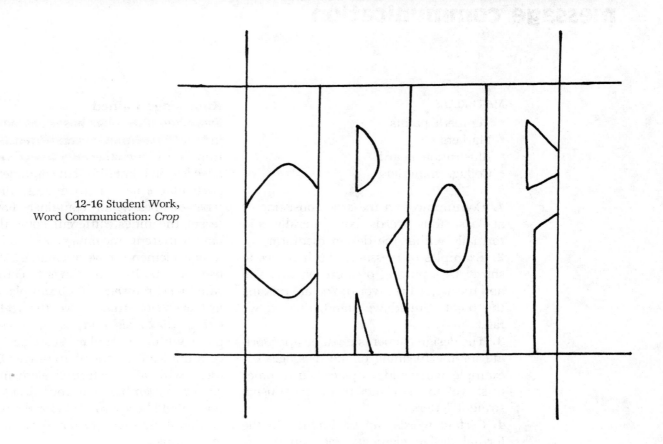

12-16 Student Work,
Word Communication: *Crop*

12-17 Alan Peckolick, typographic designer, New York,
The Informative Exchange
© Lubalin Peckolick Associates
Whenever possible, the literal message should be
communicated through the design concept.

175

message communication

MATERIALS
- Tempera paints
- Markers
- Illustration board
- Collage materials

1. Communicate a message consisting of at least four words both literally and formally within the design medium.

2. Examples of messages: Push comes to shove; He's putting pressure on me; You and me against the world; You are missing the point; United we stand, divided we fall.

3. The design elements must be appropriate for the meaning of the message. For example, we would *not* place "Push comes to shove" in the center of the page using straight letters.

4. Certain words can be implied in the formal design elements and can be excluded. The viewer will read them into the message. For example, the word *against* may be left out of the phrase. "You and me against the world" if the remaining words are positioned properly.

Knowledge Gained

Every literal message has a unique meaning. Yet that meaning can be redefined to translate it into the design medium. We have learned that different containers have particular roles or meanings, different types of lines within containers have different meanings, different color theories have different meanings, and all other design elements have meanings. We can use these built-in meanings to communicate literal messages. For example, a vertical extension might give the feeling of rising. Diagonals that set up a counterpoint within a regular rectangle help to communicate a violent message. Experiment with all the formal elements, but always remember that your design solution should be appropriate for the particular literal message. Form and meaning are inseparable.

Commercial designers must have the same knowledge of the formal elements of design as fine artists. They must also be responsive to their audience and to the

12-18 Herb Lubalin, typographic designer, *Ice Capades*, 1978, logo
© Lubalin Peckolick Associates

12-19 Student Work, Message Communication:
You're Missing the Point

12-20 Student Work, Message Communication:
In One Ear and Out the Other

177

12-21 Alan Peckolick, typographic designer, New York, logo
© Lubalin Peckolick Associates

12-22 Alan Peckolick, typographic designer, New York, logo
© Lubalin Peckolick Associates

MOTHER

12-23 Herb Lubalin, typographic designer, *Mother & Child*, 1966, logo
© Lubalin Peckolick Associates
This design has become a classic example of creative thinking. The ampersand symbolizes the embryo within the mother's womb, which is symbolized by the "O."

12-24 Alan Peckolick, typographic designer, New York, logo
© Lubalin Peckolick Associates

12-25 National Aquarium in Baltimore
Thomas H. Geismar, art director & designer
Chermayeff & Geismar Associates, New York
This simple figure/ground design of black and white curved forms conjures up images of fish in water. The design is handsome and appropriate and its simplicity lends great impact.

particular way in which the design will be read or seen. For example, we would design differently to accommodate the needs of a billboard and the needs of a magazine advertisement. There would be different considerations of scale, color, value, type, and speed of readability. Should information be designed differently for different age groups or different audiences? Yes, we must take all factors into account. The way in which people read, whether it is from left to right, right to left, or up and down, must be considered. The distance at which an audience will be reading a design message is an essential consideration as well as whether the audience will be still or in motion. How fast do we want the audience to receive the message? Scale, light and dark, color, and shape relationships are all elements we must consider as part of the communication process.

The general viewing audience is able to read symbols or pictographs as well as the written language. We all can read simple symbols of punctuation, such as *?*, *!*, and *&*. We have also come to understand that the picture of a simple geometric woman on a door, which we call a *pictograph*, means "women's wash room." Many companies and international organizations have adopted symbols to promote universal understanding. These symbols are used to break language barriers. Corporations and businesses use symbols as trademarks, believing they have staying power in the minds of consumers.

symbol design

12-26 Student Work, Symbol Design: *Peace*

MATERIALS
- Black and white tempera paint
- Illustration board
- Brush
- Pencil

1. Design a symbol or pictograph for two of the following: Food; Music; Entertainment; Sports; Peace; Civil rights; Passages; Feelings; Strength.
2. Utilize figure/ground concepts. Do not illustrate.
3. Design the space so that it is dynamic.
4. The imagery should *not* be clichés. Do many thumbnail sketches and push your ideas as far as possible.

Knowledge Gained
Symbols and pictographs are used to solve particular kinds of design problems. Design tends to be more universal than language and can serve throughout the world. Symbols are unique and have quick impact. Figure/ground design lends itself to simple, bold, and quick images.

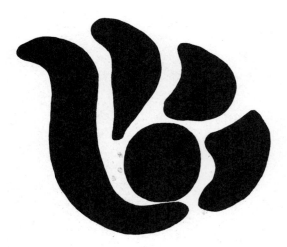

12-27 Student Work, Symbol Design: *Peace*

12-28 Student Work, Symbol Design: *Passages*

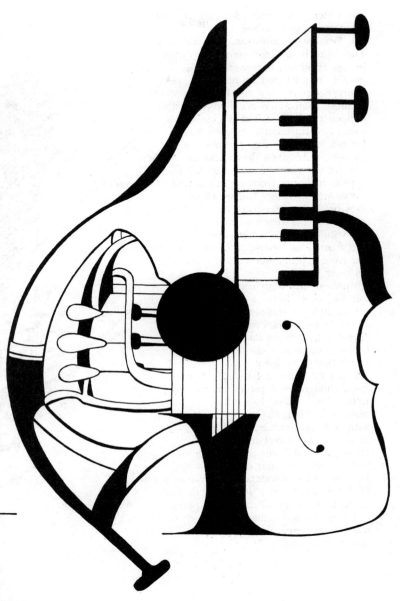

12-29 Student Work, Symbol Design: *Music*

12-30 (left) Barbara Dodsworth, calligrapher, New York
Triple E Ribbon Company, logo
The calligraphic line is appropriate for a ribbon
company. The linking of the *e*'s also relates to
a ribbonlike form.

12-31 (above) Student Work, Symbol Design: *Music*

12-32 Henry Brimmer, designer-instructor,
Academy of Art College,
San Francisco, California, *O'Plume*, logo
This logo for a down-comforter outlet
in San Francisco is powerful in its
graphic impact and its textural appeal.
Henry Brimmer: ". . . the feather was one
of those 'Hail Mary' accidents which do
happen rarely . . . I had discussed with the
client two different directions to go
for her logo: One was the obvious
connection between down and the feather.
The second was a more illustrative
approach drawn from an old German children's
story, *Mother Holle.* Mother Holle
lives up in heaven, every morning she
shakes out her down comforter out
the window, on earth it snows. . . .
We wanted to stay away from geese since
her major competitor uses the goose
on their logo.
To present her with roughs I asked
her for some down. I spent too much time
on the Mother Holle approach and
twenty minutes before presentation, I
threw a feather on the lens board of
a stat camera and clicked it—the
result being the logo!
When I first saw it I thought it was
good enough for a presentation, [and]
if the client would like it I'd
reshoot it. Well, the client loved its
simplicity and chose it over the
Mother Holle. I reshot it about fifty
times and could not get a better
version than the first one.
I do show my students my work, and when
O'Plume comes up I do point out that
sometimes the accident does happen,
but that usually it takes a bit
more time, research, and effort to
arrive at a solution."

182

glossary

Acrylic paint: A synthetic water-based paint that is available in tubes or jars.

Activate: To create tensions or energy on a surface.

After-image: The involuntary color or shape seen by the human eye after the exhaustion of certain receptors in the eye.

Analogous colors: Colors that are adjacent to one another on the geometric color wheel.

Asymmetry: The lack of symmetry.

Atomsphere: The illusion of air-filled space on a two-dimensional surface.

Atmospheric perspective: The representation of a spatial effect on a two-dimensional surface that takes into account the effect the atmosphere has on color, form, and detail. Also called *aerial perspective.*

Balance: The harmonious arrangement of elements in a work of art.

Baroque art: The period of art in Western Europe from c. 1580 to c. 1720.

Blottings: An indirect mark made by dipping interesting objects or surfaces in ink or paint and blotting them on a two-dimensional surface.

Casein paints: Paint in which casein, a powdered protein made from milk, is used as a binder.

Chroma: The relative intensity of a hue. A hue can be bright or dull, weak or strong.

Closed: A self-contained unbroken form.

Collage: The technique of cutting and pasting materials to the surface of a page or canvas.

Color-Aid paper: A manufactured series of colored papers.

Color weight: The quality of a color, hue, value, chroma, opacity, and transparency that determines its apparent position in space.

Color wheel: A system of ordering hues from which we derive color theories.

Complements: Hues that are opposite one another on the color wheel.

Complex compounds: Hues that are mixtures of compound hues with either primaries or secondaries—for example, GYG or RVR.

183

Composition: The arrangement of forms to constitute a unit.

Compound hues: Hues that are mixtures between primaries and secondaries—for example, YG or RV.

Compressed vision: The representation of a wide or long expanse of vision on a regular rectangle.

Conceptual: Art that is derived solely from the mind and *not* from the process of looking at things in the real world.

Concrete: Art that remains flat; true to the nature of the two-dimensional surface.

Container: The borders of the page or canvas, which can be a variety of different shapes. There are regular rectangles, squares, tondos, vertical extensions, horizontal extensions, and shaped containers.

Cropped imagery: The cutting of an image to make the image or form seem larger or closer.

Cubism: An art movement in the early twentieth-century led by Pablo Picasso and Georges Braque in France.

Curvilinear: A form characterized by curving lines.

Diagonal: A line that moves in an oblique direction.

Direct mark: A mark made directly by the artist using tools such as pens, pencils, markers, or brushes, as opposed to indirect marks.

Dynamic lines: Lines that contrast the borders of a container.

Element: The elements in design are: line, color, shape, texture, the container, volume, space, balance, focal point, symmetry, asymmetry, and light and shadow.

Empirical: Knowledge gained through a method based on first-hand experience, observation, or trial and error.

Entry: The area in a design or painting that invites our eye into the space.

Extended triad: The addition of analogous hues to either the major or minor triad.

Extended vision: The vertical or horizontal expanse of our vision.

Field: The visual expanse of a surface.

Field density: The appearance of heavy atmosphere on a two-dimensional surface.

Figure/ground design: The equal treatment of forms on a flat surface so that no one form is dominant.

Focal point: The point to which the viewer's eyes are directed through compositional means.

Form: A generic term referring to the artist's representation of almost anything, including abstraction, and excluding subject.

Formal: The elements in design that define design as a medium: line, color, shape, light and shadow, and so on. The formal elements in a design or picture are all those with the exclusion of the subject matter.

Gradation: A color scale where the value range goes from light to dark.

Ground: The background, in contrast to the key or figure, which is forward in the space. Also, the support painted onto a surface to support the pigment.

Harmony: In color, an agreeable arrangement of hues, values, and chromas which could stem from a specific color theory.

Hatching: The creation of value or shadow by applying closely spaced parallel lines. Crosshatching is defined as one group of hatched lines crossing another group of hatched lines in a different direction.

Horizontal: A line parallel to the horizon, a movement from side to side as opposed to an up and down movement.

Horizontal extension: A rectangle that is prolonged in a horizontal direction.

Hue: The specific name of a color, such as blue, red, yellow-green, or yellow-orange.

Iconography: The use of symbols and recognizable images to convey a meaning that is not necessarily evident upon surface examination.

Illusion: The appearance of three-dimensional space on a two-dimensional surface.

Impressionism: An art movement in France during the nineteenth century led by artists such as Monet, Degas, and Renoir.

Indirect marks: In contrast to direct marks, marks made by an intervening stage, as in printmaking, rubbing, or blotting.

Isolation: The creation of a point of focus by isolating a form or color on a page.

Key: The forward figure on a page placed on top of the ground.

Layout: The organization of graphic space in design.

Linear: As opposed to *painterly*, the quality of design in which forms are expressed primarily by the use of both contour and interior line.

Major triad: The hues red, yellow, and blue, which are formed by inscribing an equilateral triangle in the geometric color wheel.

Matte medium: A liquid used to thin synthetic colors or increase fluidity, which results in a matte or semimat effect.

Medium: A developed system with which we can communicate meanings and feelings.

Minor triad: The hues orange, violet, and green, which are formed by inscribing an equilateral triangle in the geometric color wheel.

Narrative art: In art, the telling of a story.

Object oriented: Viewing objects as separate from one another as opposed to seeing them as having unity or connection.

Opaque: A color that is not see-through, not translucent.

Optical art: A twentieth century movement that employs the use of design and/or color to create strong optical illusions of motion, depth, and volume on the two-dimensional surface.

Optical mixture: The visual merging of color in visual perception.

Orphism: An artistic movement related to Cubism that stressed color relationships. The movement was led by Robert Delaunay in France in the early twentieth century.

Painterly: In contrast to *linear*, the expression of form in which line is ostensibly dissolved and three-dimensions are created by the use of color and light.

Parallelism: A compositional method of organizing elements to create similar rhythms or movements.

Perceptual: The gathering of information from things directly observed in nature.

Perspective: The schematic representation of three-dimensional objects on a two-dimensional surface.

Pictograph: Public symbols used for international purposes.

Picture plane: The surface of the page or canvas that can be manipulated forward or backward depending upon the degree of illusionism in the picture.

Placement: The position of elements on a page.

Plane: A flat surface.

Point of view: The particular vantage point established in a design or painting, a strategic positioning of elements by the artist.

Positive/negative space: A synonym for figure/ground space or design.

Post-Impressionism: A generic term for art movements that came after Impressionism and that, in some way, reacted to the art of the Impressionists. Some Post-Impressionist artists are Paul Cézanne, Vincent van Gogh, and Georges Seurat.

Primary colors: Hues that cannot be made from any other colors. They are red, yellow, and blue in pigment.

Push and pull of color: The manipulation of the position of color in space on a two-dimensional surface.

Recessional space: The illusion of three-dimensions moving back behind the picture plane.

Regular rectangle: A rectangle that is not extremely prolonged in either a vertical or horizontal direction.

Renaissance art: A period of art from c. 1400 to c. 1550 that was concerned with the revival of classical ideals.

Render: To illustratively depict.

Rubbings: The creation of an image made by rubbing a pencil or crayon on paper which is held over a textured object.

Sans-serif letter: The most simplified letter form available without any extraneous components, as opposed to serif letters.

Scale: The relative qualities of size in relation to both space and relative position.

Scroll: Any painting or manuscript done on long rolled cloth, paper, or skins.

Secondary colors: Hues that are mixtures of two of the primaries. They are orange, green, and violet.

Serif letters: As opposed to sans-serif letters, a small graphic addition to the bodies of letters in typography.

Split complement: A pair of complements that has one of its components split to include its immediate analogous hues and exclude the component that has been split. It is a color theory derived from the geometric color wheel.

Static line: A line that repeats the edges of the container.

Symbol: A mark or image used to identify a corporation, agency, institution, or idea.

Symmetry: Identical mirror images on either side of a vertical axis.

Tactile: The depiction of an object or texture in two-dimensions that strongly appeals to the sense of touch.

Tempera paint: In modern times, any opaque water paint such as poster colors, gouache colors, and simple casein paint.

Thumbnail sketches: Small quick sketches used to rough out ideas.

Tondo: A circular container.

Tone: A synonym for value.

Translucent: A see-through color.

Type: Mechanically produced letters having consistent design qualities.

Typeface: A particular species of type.

Typography: Graphic design employing type and any use of type including design, display lettering, and hand-modified lettering.

Underlying structure: The composition of a design or painting.

Up-front space: Space that is compressed toward the front part of a picture or design.

Value: The relative lightness or darkness of a hue.

Vertical: A line perpendicular to the horizon, moving in an up and down direction.

Vertical extension: A container that is prolonged in a vertical direction.

Volume: The three-dimensional qualities of a two-dimensional image.

Warp: The appearance of a shift in the surface of a page or canvas.

suggested readings

Albers, Josef. *The Interaction of Color.* New Haven and London: Yale University Press, 1963.

Brown, David. *The Annual of the American Institute of Graphic Arts:USA 2.* New York: Watson-Guptill Publications, 1981.

Clark, Kenneth. *Civilization.* New York: Harper & Row, 1969.

Donahue, Bud. *The Language of Layout.* Englewood Cliffs, N.J.: Prentice-Hall, 1978.

Gentille, T. *Printed Textiles: A Guide to Creative Design Fundamentals.* Englewood Cliffs, N.J.: Prentice-Hall, 1982.

Griffith, Thomas. *A Practical Guide for Beginning Painters.* Englewood Cliffs, N.J.: Prentice-Hall, 1981.

Herdeg, Walter, ed. *Araphis Annual 81/82.* Zurich, Switzerland: Graphis Press Corp.

Hurlburt, Allen. *Publication Design.* New York: Van Nostrand Reinhold Co., 1969.

Leslie, Clare Walker. *Nature Drawing: A Tool for Learning.* Englewood Cliffs, N.J.: Prentice-Hall, 1980.

Mussell, Albert. *A Grammar of Color.* Faber Birren, ed. New York: Van Nostrand Reinhold Co., 1969.

Simmons, Seymour III, and Winer, Mark S.A. *Drawing: The Creative Process.* Englewood Cliffs, N.J.: Prentice-Hall, 1977.

Thoma, Marta. *Graphic Illustration: Tools and Techniques for Beginning Illustrators.* Englewood Cliffs, N.J.: Prentice-Hall, 1982.

index